# *In Female Worth and Elegance*

*Sampler worked in 1840 by Sarah Emily Currier. Collections of the Portsmouth Historical Society. Dan Gair photograph.*

# *In Female Worth and Elegance*

*Sampler and Needlework Students and Teachers in Portsmouth, New Hampshire, 1741–1840*

## John F. LaBranche
## Rita F. Conant

**The Portsmouth Marine Society**

*Publication Twenty-Two*

*Published for the Society by*

Peter E. Randall
PUBLISHER

*Designed and produced by*
*Peter E. Randall Publisher*
*Box 4726, Portsmouth, NH 03802*

*A publication of*
*The Portsmouth Marine Society*
*Box 147, Portsmouth, NH 03802*

*ISBN 0915819-21-X*

———————

*ISBN10: 0915819-37-6*
*ISBN13: 978-0-915819-37-9*

———————

*To Richard Conant,*
*Brenda LaBranche, and*
*Abigail LaBranche*

———————

*To Jean Sawtelle whose collecting of*
*Portsmouth samplers continues to inform*
*our knowledge of women's needlework*
*in early Portsmouth*

*and*

*Merrilee Possner whose bequest made possible*
*the conservation and remounting of the*
*Portsmouth Historical Society samplers*

# Contents

# Exhibition Checklist of Samplers

*May 23-October 31, 2009*

*The second edition of this book is published in conjunction with a new exhibit by the Portsmouth Historical Society entitled "Stitches in Time: Portsmouth Samplers 1765-1840" held at the John Paul Jones House. The exhibit consists of several vignettes arranged chronologically to place these local samplers in a cultural context with related portraits, furniture, silver and ceramics associated with the makers.*

| OWNERS | SAMPLE CREATORS |
|---|---|
| *Portsmouth Historical Society* | Sally Breed |
| | Caroline Currier |
| | Sarah Emily Currier |
| | Ann Pierce Drown (2 samplers) |
| | Mary Frances Folsom |
| | Elizabeth Gilman |
| | Sarah Hart |
| | Mary Harvey |
| | Harriet Langdon |
| | Deborah Laighton |
| | Elizabeth Lake |
| | Sarah Sherburne |
| | Susan Stodder |
| | Elizabeth Fabyan Willey |
| *Shirley-Eustis Mansion* | Caroline Langdon |
| *Louise Richardson* | Mehitable Frost |

*Jean Sawtelle*    Mary Greenleaf Clark
Elizabeth Cutter
Harriet Ann Dockum
Mary Catherine Evans
Elizabeth Fernald
Ann Elizabeth Ham
Almira Hilton
Hannah Langdon
Mary Lonergan
Mary Ann Marden
Sarah Elizabeth Marden
Caroline Odiorne
Eliza Jane Salter
Mary Augusta Shapleigh
Lucretia Tarlton

# Acknowledgments, Second Edition

Our thanks to the Portsmouth Marine Society and Peter Randall for publishing this second edition. Jean Sawtelle has greatly aided our exhibit "Stitches in Time: Portsmouth Samplers 1765-1840" by lending her collection of Portsmouth samplers. A bequest from Merrilee Possner made it possible to conserve and properly mount the samplers in the Portsmouth Historical Society collection.

We also recognize our colleagues at Strawbery Banke, the Moffat Ladd House, the Warner House, the Wentworth-Gardner and Tobias Lear House Association and the Portsmouth Athenaeum for their joint effort in creating "Through the Eye of the Needle," a group of exhibitions featuring Portsmouth needlework during the 2009 season. "Stitches in Time: Portsmouth Samplers 1765-1840" is the Portsmouth Historical Society's contribution to this season honoring Portsmouth needlework.

The following individuals and businesses have helped to create "Stitches in Time: Portsmouth Samplers 1765-1840." Stephanie Rohwer, Portsmouth Historical Society intern, assisted with writing labels, publicity and assembling the exhibit. Ursula Wright, Portsmouth Historical Society curator, assisted with research on local families and editing exhibit labels. Northeast Auctions assisted by providing a professional image of the Deborah Leighton sampler and Alan Haesche photographed the Portsmouth Historical Society samplers. The Shirley Eustis House Association kindly lent Caroline Langdon Eustis's sampler and Louise Richardson has lent a newly discovered Portsmouth sampler by Mehitable Frost. Nina Rayer and Virginia Whelen provided needed conservation work and Framing Alternative provided new frames for the remounted samplers.

Sandra Rux, Collections Manager
Portsmouth Historical Society

# Introduction, Second Edition

The impetus for this second edition of *In Female Worth and Elegance* was the opportunity to create a new exhibition featuring locally stitched samplers by the Portsmouth Historical Society at its John Paul Jones House. Although "Stitches in Time: Portsmouth Samplers 1765–1840" has a slightly different focus than the 1996 exhibit at the Portsmouth Athenäeum, the book is a comprehensive overview of Portsmouth's needlework creators and their teachers. As this essential reference document has long been out of print and hard to find, it seemed important to produce a second edition. The text and index of this second edition of *In Female Worth and Elegance* remains exactly as the first. Color images and their captions have been changed, however, to allow us to add several samplers not found in the first edition and to change photo credits where the older images were not available.

While *In Female Worth and Elegance* focuses on the relationship between the needlework schools, teachers and students, the exhibition "Stitches in Time" concentrates on the relationships of these works to other objects owned by the sampler makers or their families. Related objects such as portraits, furniture, ceramics and other needlework examples have been combined to place the samplers in a domestic context over the period 1765 to 1840. This was only possible because the Portsmouth Historical Society collection includes so many items from the same families as the sampler makers—often donated to the Society at the same time. It also contains a number of objects related to samplers in the Sawtelle collection.

Without the useful research behind *In Female Worth and Elegance*, we could not have made the many connections between objects and samplers. We hope a second edition will make this basic information more available to museums and individuals who own or collect these samplers and to all those who have not yet been able to find a copy of the book.

As a collecting institution, the Portsmouth Historical Society hopes this new edition helps readers to identify more samplers made in eighteenth and nineteenth century Portsmouth. If so, we would greatly appreciate learning of those samplers not identified in these pages.

# Acknowledgments

WE ARE ESPECIALLY indebted to needlework historians Betty Ring, Susan Swan, Mary Jaene Edmonds, Glee Kruger, and Louise Woodhead Feuerstein for their frequent advice and continual encouragement and to Nancy Goss and Joan Stephens for their willing support of this project.

We have also valued the assistance of the docents at the Warner House and the Portsmouth Historical Society, who oversee a rich array of Portsmouth needleworks, and to Carolyn Roy, assistant curator at Strawbery Banke Museum, who assisted us in authenticating examples in their collections.

At the Newington Historical Society we received enthusiastic help from Barbara Myers, who permitted us access to their collection and provided information concerning the Langdon and Gaines samplers housed there.

Among the collectors of needlework who lent a helping hand are Jean Sawtelle, Kevin Nicolson, and Sheila Rideout.

We are very grateful to the descendants of a number of the needleworkers who have graciously given us access to information and needlework and often provided photographs. They include William Peter Coues, Mrs. Merrill Ten Broeck Spalding, Mrs. John Lear, Miss Serena Jones, Paul Lindsay, and John Bradford, who is curator of the Shirley-Eustis Mansion in Roxbury, Massachusetts.

Our thanks go to the research librarians at the Portsmouth Public Library, the Old York Historical Society, and the Maine State Library as well as to Margaret Morse, librarian and curator of the

Allegheny College special collections at Meadville, Pennsylvania. We owe a special thanks to Special Collections librarian Carolyn Eastman at the Portsmouth Athenaeum for calling to our attention manuscripts relating to the Coues, Parrott, and Spalding families. Thanks are owed, as well, to Donna Bell Garvin at the New Hampshire Historical Society for assistance with research on George Dame.

Without the support and help of Joseph and Jean Sawtelle, this book would not have been possible, and without the boundless patience and skillful expertise of publisher Peter Randall the project may very well have been shelved long ago. We are grateful for their willingness to underwrite this publication.

Of course, we are also grateful for the love and support of our families.

John F. LaBranche and Rita F. Conant
Kittery, Maine
November, 1996

# Introduction

IT WAS THE 1822 sampler worked by the hands of seven-year-old Lucy Maria Wiggin that at first delighted and ultimately inspired us to want to learn more about the needlework of Portsmouth, New Hampshire. Once discovered, this fetching example of Portsmouth schoolgirl art started us on a quest for others. The search was always fruitful and amazing and provided us with an enlightening glimpse into the social and economic history of late-eighteenth- and early-nineteenth century life on the New Hampshire seacoast.

Lucy's sampler conforms to a style long associated with Portsmouth needlework. The house, fence, birdhouse, and barn—very often flanked by generous baskets of mounded fruit—and the rendering of the alphabet, numerals, and a verse make up the unmistakable format. Samplers were often stitched on a green linsey-woolsey ground. At the outset of our investigation, only about a half dozen such examples were known to exist. Since so few documented Portsmouth needleworks had surfaced over the years, other than those recorded by Ethel Stanwood Bolton and Eva Johnston Coe in their 1921 landmark work, *American Samplers*, along with a handful in museum collections, we had only modest hopes of locating and authenticating others.

But what soon began to unfold for us was a more complete and fascinating slice of Portsmouth life than we had ever imagined we might uncover. As the evidence mounted, we were forced to set 1840 as the cutoff date for what was becoming a lengthy list of students and teachers. Ultimately the trail led to more than a hundred students and over a hundred teachers in the period 1741 to 1840.

*Sampler worked by Lucy Maria Wiggin in 1822. Courtesy of Strawbery Banke Museum.*

Instruction in needlework played an important role in the education of Portsmouth females well into the nineteenth century. Judged on technical merit, the work of these young students (the average age of the girls is eleven) exhibits a range of capabilities. We found no boys among the lists of needlework students or on the samplers with a Portsmouth provenance.

Perhaps the most interesting discovery is that several of the later works—those done between 1830 and 1840—display the finest workmanship. This seems all the more surprising given the generally held opinion that overall the needlework from this period exhibits a strong decline in quality.

In 1793 John Cosens Ogden, then rector of St. John's Episcopal Church in Portsmouth, penned his treatise entitled *The Female Guide,* in which he declared, "The needle and distaff may be early put into the management of females, and go hand in hand with the important branches of reading, writing, arithmetic, accounts, geography, history and poetry."[1]

This was by no means the first time the majority of Portsmouth's citizens had heard the theory put forth. Ogden, indeed, had to confess at the outset that, "This theme has been discussed so often, that I cannot insure you that I shall say anything new."[2]

Sermons, treatises, discourses, and newspaper items on the subject appeared with great regularity by the final decade of the eighteenth century. The *New Hampshire Gazette and General Advertiser* of May 5, 1790, carried an anonymous ode entitled "Parnassian Spring/On Female Education," which advocated instruction in elocution, grammar, vocabulary, geography, and mathematics for females, concluding:

> yet to my weak brains it seemeth/ more strange,/ Your fathers were all once such fools./ As ignorant wives to take for their lives—/ And many yet follow their rules.[3]

Not everyone, it seems, had been sold on a dubious philosophy that placed so much knowledge into the hands of women.

The prototype for Ogden's *Guide* appeared some six years earlier in Philadelphia when a prominent physician and signer of the Declaration of Independence, Dr. Benjamin Rush, issued his *Thoughts on Female Education, Accommodated to the Present State of Society, Manners and Government in the U.S.A.*[4] Rush advocated a plan based on a theory of female education that would help ensure the stability of the American family and ultimately the nation by distributing basic knowledge more liberally between the sexes.[5]

The uncertainties of the day-to-day circumstances during the Revolutionary War years in particular and the privations experienced by almost every family heightened the sense of urgency to make women more equal in their marriage partnerships. The objective was to prepare women for coping with change, sudden or otherwise, in their circumstances. Such preparedness could not be born of ignorance; there existed a real sense that much work remained to be done in the education of females.

So Portsmouth, like almost every other city and town along the eastern seaboard, found itself swept up in this new wave of support for the education of young misses. Portsmouth clergymen and educators, men like Rev. John Cosens Ogden, the Rev. Dr. Samuel Haven, Rev. Timothy Alden, Rev. Charles Burroughs, Benjamin Dearborn, and the Rev. Dr. Joseph Buckminster, in turn delivered their orations in support of a more progressive attitude toward female education. Some orators waxed more eloquently and more often than others but by and large they all subscribed to Dr. Rush's 1787 plan.

While Ogden was most disposed to turning a well-constructed phrase, Rev. Timothy Alden, after a single flash of oratorical genius in 1801, displayed what must have been an annoying propensity for wandering off into lengthy and oblique ramblings, employing every biblical maxim at his command.[6] One can only imagine that there were waves of nodding heads to be seen at Portsmouth's South Church on those occasions between 1800 and 1805 when Alden occupied the pulpit. Still, it was Alden who operated one of the most successful academies for young masters and misses during this time. He included needlework as an important part of the curriculum and his school has proved to be the only one from which we can identify silk pictures worked in Portsmouth both by student and by subject.

Regardless of their individual oratory skills, the message was the same: A more stable society, a stronger family unit, and to some degree freedom from want for women who suddenly found themselves in distressed means could be had for the price of a well-rounded education.

Ogden expressed the philosophy quite clearly:

By instructing our Females in those useful and necessary branches of industry which are peculiar to their sex the use of the needle in particular we also furnish them with a source of wealth and profit, which is necessary for all conditions of life; which may be laid aside when affluence permits, or assumed when adversity with its billow rolls trouble and indigence upon them. Were the opulent only impressed with the uncertainty of riches, how suddenly they may flee way; and were the poor instructed in the various branches of female industry, both would escape one half the miseries of life.[7]

Charles Burroughs, who by 1827 had succeeded Ogden at St.

John's, carried the essence of this plan of education to its most logical and perhaps most important conclusions: "The importance of female education," he wrote, "will be readily admitted, if we advert to that powerful moral influence, which women hold over their children."[8] The outcome of such a system of education then produced beneficial effects that have positive consequences for generations to come.

The number of schools offering instruction for young misses, both public and private, expanded most rapidly during the first quarter of the nineteenth century. Many included instruction in needlework, and the private schools in particular, as we will see, took great care to offer as wide a variety of choices in this area as possible. As enthusiasm for the establishment of a strong new republic gained momentum, the Rev. Timothy Alden penned a telling description of a Portsmouth poised to stride forward into a future almost universally viewed as filled with boundless promise.

> On the banks of the Piscataqua we are favored with one of the most pleasant situations in America.
>
> We have one of the best harbors in the United States. Our mercantile and commercial interests are in a very prosperous condition. We know of no town, where greater encouragement is given to the mechanic.
>
> Among the most distinguished improvements, which have here marked the close of the eighteenth century, we may mention the new market; the number of elegant houses lately erected; the aqueduct; and the beautiful rows of the Lombardy poplar, which begin to appear.[9]

*The Reverend Timothy Alden circa 1835. Artist unknown. Courtesy of Allegheny College, Meadville, Pennsylvania. Bill Owen photograph.*

# The Portsmouth Teachers

*'Tis education forms the common mind*
*Just as the twig is bent the tree's inclined.*[10]

**D**OUBTLESS ALEXANDER POPE (1688–1744) never intended his heroic couplet as verse for the samplers of young misses. Yet it found its way not only into cross-stitch but into the masthead of ads for schools as well.

"Schools and academies so universally abound," wrote the Rev. Timothy Alden in his famous 1801 sermon, "that it may be said, in no part of the world is the education of both sexes, of every description, upon a better footing than in America."[11] Pope's couplet ideally suited the prevailing feeling toward the education of America's youngsters, including females. Most frequently advertisements offered instruction for both sexes, with classes for females given in separate rooms or at alternate times of the day. Schools run by women invariably included instruction in the "useful and ornamental" arts—needlework, painting, and drawing, for instance. Male instructors frequently engaged the services of a preceptress to provide instruction in needlework.

Certainly, by the final quarter of the eighteenth century, the citizens of Portsmouth had developed a genuine appetite for educating their daughters. David McClure, teaching here in 1773, made this entry in his diary: "Opened school, consisting the first day of about 30 Misses. Afterward they increased to 70 or 80; so that I was obliged to divide the day between them and one half came in the forenoon and the other in the afternoon. They were from 7 to 20 years of age."[12]

1

Despite the obvious success of his school, McClure does not appear to have stayed in Portsmouth long, preferring, perhaps, to move on to more fertile fields.

In many respects education for the public at large became as much a business endeavor as it was an undertaking of positive social impact. Competition among teachers was keen and while the number of schools advertised multiplied steadily, most vanished after only a single season in operation. The successful schools and academies—those that lasted more than three or four years—were few in number. They were schools run by members of the clergy, like the Rev. Timothy Alden, or prominent citizens such as Benjamin Dearborn, George Dame, or family endeavors such as those of Samuel and Amos Tappan or Daniel Austin and his sister Sarah.

Many of the women who appeared fleetingly on the scene as teachers were recent widows or without kin and simply needed to support themselves. Mary Ann Weare Swett Kenney helped support herself through the loss of three husbands and what must have been increasingly demanding economic straits. Her ads appear with regularity from 1814 through 1822 and the inventory of her mariner husband James Kenney's estate, made in September 1822, included "School Benches 2.50."[13]

Without question the most successful institutions offering instruction to young misses were those operated by Benjamin Dearborn and the Reverend Alden. It was in 1780 that Dearborn opened a school for misses at his house on Paved Street, where he taught reading, spelling, writing, and arithmetic.[14] Sometime later he had a separate building erected at the back of his house, and on April 30, 1791, the *New Hampshire Gazette* reported, "Last Monday at the opening of Mr. Dearborn's Academy the Hall was so crowded as to oblige him to adjourn the performances to the Rev. Mr. Buckminster's meeting house, where a very large concourse of people assembled on the occasion." The Rev. John Ogden of St. John's Church delivered a discourse and the Rev. Samuel Haven of South Church composed an ode for the occasion in which he praised "Female Worth and Elegance."

Dearborn's academy had, by this time, been in existence for over ten years and was perhaps the first major institution of its kind in Portsmouth to have attended to the education of young misses of the merchant classes. Over the years his curriculum expanded from reading, spelling, writing, and arithmetic to include "a Master to teach the French Language and Dancing." Interestingly, though, he engaged the services of a preceptress to instruct in "the useful and ornamental branches of needlework" only six months before his academy closed.[15]

Late in September 1791, Dearborn announced that "on account of support being withdrawn from some of the branches of instruction in Portsmouth Academy and given to rival institutions, [I am] obliged to discontinue said Academy, from the 1st of October."[16] It may well have been that Dearborn succumbed to the mounting pressures of increased competition from others on the scene but it seems more likely that he decided to seek his fortune elsewhere. He left Portsmouth for Boston, where he established a new academy in the Green Dragon building in Union Street.[17]

While there were a number of "schools" offering instruction for young ladies in the final decade of the eighteenth century, advertisements for them were rare. Among the few to be found were those placed by Samuel Tappan and Amos Tappan. At first, the pair operated independently, but by mid-decade they had joined forces to form a school that continued to advertise through 1802.

The Tappan school taught the customary array of subjects appropriate for females and employed a woman to instruct the misses in needlework. What seems most revealing about their convictions with respect to educating young women is reflected clearly in the 1821 will of Amos Tappan:

> I give and bequeath to my dearly beloved child Eliza Tappan the sum of five hundred dollars as small compensation for the abundant and faithful service rendered to my family during many years past, and I take this opportunity to express my satisfaction and approbation of her dutiful conduct and behavior. I give and bequeath to my dearly beloved child Mary Lyman Buckminster five dollars in books to be selected by Rev. Mr. Putnam.[18]

Here is a vivid example of the true thrust of female education through the "useful and ornamental" arts. Despite her education, Mary's legacy came in the form of a collection of books to be selected by her minister. Her father's library contained some one hundred thirty volumes probably representing one of the larger private libraries in Portsmouth at the time. Eliza, following in the footsteps of countless others, carried out her role as daughter and family attendant both admirably and stoically, it would appear.

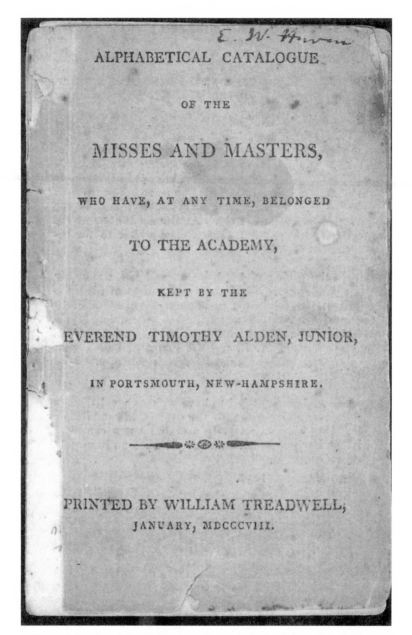

ALPHABETICAL CATALOGUE

OF THE

MISSES AND MASTERS,

WHO HAVE, AT ANY TIME, BELONGED

TO THE ACADEMY,

KEPT BY THE

EVEREND TIMOTHY ALDEN, JUNIOR,

IN PORTSMOUTH, NEW-HAMPSHIRE.

PRINTED BY WILLIAM TREADWELL,
JANUARY, MDCCCVIII.

*Cover (above) and first two pages (opposite) of catalog of students who attended the academy kept by Reverend Timothy Alden Jr. Published in Portsmouth in 1808.  Private collection.*

## MEMORANDUM.

Mr. Alden commenced his ACADEMY in Portsmouth, for misses only, in the spring of 1800. He kept it most of the time after, except in the wintry season, till he had concluded on a disconnection with his parochial charge. This event took place on the twelfth of August, 1805. At the solicitation of his friends, he devoted the ensuing winter to the instruction of misses.

In the spring of 1806, he opened his ACADEMY for both sexes. Since the enlargement of his institution, the following gentlemen have, at different times, aided him in the business of instruction, David Tappan, A. B. deacon Enoch M. Clarke, and William Weeks, A. B. and the following ladies, miss Margaret Cushing, miss Elizabeth Allen, and miss Sarah Cogswell.

Mr. Alden intended to have written a valedictory address, appropriate to the use of his pupils, on bringing his ACADEMY to a close ; but a crowd of cares has precluded him the pleasure and the pain of such a task.

20 January, 1808.

## MISSES.

Elizabeth Adams.
Anna Maria Adams.
Sarah Adams.
Ann Hall Adams.
Martha Wright Alden.
Elizabeth Shepherd Wormsted Alden.
Charlotte King Atkinson, Dover.
Susan Sparhawk Atkinson, Dover.
Maria Penhallow Austin.
Sarah Wentworth Austin.
Myra Ayers, Canterbury.
Ann Bagnell, St. Vincent.
Margaret Bagnell, St. Vincent.
Elizabeth Amory Bagnell, St. Vincent.
Ann Palmer Bagnell, St. Vincent.
Mary Stevenson Bailey.
Abigail Bailard, Durham.
Elizabeth Gove Bean.
Louisa Blasdel.
Mary Ann Blunt.
Eleanor Sherburne Blunt.
Sarah Blunt.
Elizabeth Blunt,
Ann Boardman.

REVEREND MR. ALDEN'S ACADEMY,

AT PORTSMOUTH,

FOR THE INSTRUCTION OF MASTERS AND MISSES

IN VARIOUS BRANCHES OF USEFUL

KNOWLEDGE.

CATALOGUE OF PUPILS FOR THE QUARTER ENDING XIII JANUARY, MDCCCVII.

FIRST CLASS OF MASTERS.

— William Manning. 4 Jan. 141. Charles Yeaton.8-c-c-c. 33. John Parker Flagg.

206. Benjamin Franklin Salter.2-c-c-c-c-c. — Daniel Jackson. 29 Dec. SECOND CLASS OF MASTERS.

— John Brewster Gerrish.1- 31. John Greenleaf.3-

8 Dec. — John Swett.1- 59. John Hale Sheafe.c- — Hall Jackson Tibbitts.2-

44. Charles Joseph Sergent, 4 Nov. 20. Messidor Tuscan. 25. George Blunt.2-

— Oliver Sheafe.6-

FIRST CLASS OF MISSES.

170. Mehetabel Coats Greenleaf.1-c-c-c-c-c. 253. Ann Hall Adams.2-c-c-c-c-c-c-c. 70. Sarah Blunt.

8 Jan. — Sarah Adams Norton. 28. Mary Ann Hacker.p- 198. Elizabeth Epes Carter.3-c-c-c-c-c-c.

— Mary Ann Low, 57. Frances Shea.2- 50. Adeline Haven.2-

244. Mercy Jackson.2-p-c-c-c-c-c-c-c-c. 58. Mary Ann Shapley.1-c- 36. Elizabeth Hamilton Clarke.?-

23 Nov.— Mary Thompson. 122. Elizabeth Wentworth Haven.2-c-c-c. 21. Charlotte Ann Haven.c-

— Sarah Ann Manning. 249. Elizabeth Sewall Goddard.3-c-c-c-c-c-c-c-c. 16. Sarah Sherburne Langdon.

69. Frances Dorothy Wentworth Sherburne.c-c- SECOND CLASS OF MISSES. THIRD CLASS OF MISSES.

5 Jan. — Lydia Norton. 14. Catharine Hammond Melcher.1-c- 23. Mary Tarlton Libbey.1-

249. Lucy Maria Goddard.1-c-c-c-c-c-c-c. 50. Frances Amory Langdon. 20. Mary Catharine Sergent.2-

26. Elizabeth Hill Jones, — Catharine Staters.c- 27. Elizabeth Blunt.1-c-

85. Eleanor Sherburne Blunt.c-p-c- 50. Margaret Newman Hewes.3-c- 42. Martha Wright Alden.1-c-

25. Mary Ann Hall.p-c- 19 Dec. 14. Jane Boyd Mackay.c- 32. Harriet Bradbury Clarke.3-

— Abigail Bowles. 42. Lucy Seaward.c-m- — Elizabeth Shepherd Wormsted Alden.

66. Caroline Haven.2-c-c-

Those, who recite lessons memoriter, are considered as performing well, if they repeat with correctness twenty lines, at a time, from DOCTOR MORSE'S ABRIDGMENT OF GEOGRAPHY, or their equivalent in any other book used for this purpose. In this certificate, a quarto page of composition is also considered as equal to a lesson. The number of lessons, with which the pupils were accredited, on this plan, in course of the quarter, which ended 13 January, 1807, is designated by the figures prefixed to their names respectively. It is the custom at this institution, for the pupils of the several classes to take their places, from day to day, according to their respective performance of certain tasks, which are assigned them. Once a week, the head of each class receives an honorary certificate. The figures suffixed to certain names, in the foregoing catalogue, point out those, who have arrived at this mark of distinction, and the number of times, during the quarter. As a further stimulus to a laudable ambition, an honorary certificate is also conferred upon each pupil, who learns and repeats twenty lessons in a week. Every certificate granted for this performance is pointed out by the letter c, added to the names of the successful candidates. The letter c is added to the names of those, who embroider, m to the names of those, who work muslin, and p to the names of those, who attend to painting. Dates are placed before the names of those, who entered a considerable time after the quarter was begun. Those, whose names are subjoined, are considered as having particularly excelled during the quarter now closed, in arithmetick and in this order.

MASTERS. MISSES. Ann Hall Adams.

William Manning, Lucy Maria Goddard. Elizabeth Wentworth Haven.

Charles Yeaton, Mercy Jackson, Elizabeth Sewall Goddard.

During the quarter just closed, miss Eleanor Sherburne Blunt and miss Elizabeth Wentworth Haven have finished repeating memoriter select parts of MASON'S SELF KNOWLEDGE to the amount of two thousand eight hundred and ninety lines.
Miss Isabella Shapley Fernald has finished repeating memoriter a treatise composed by the reverend Charles Stearns, of Lincoln, entitled PRINCIPLES OF RELIGION AND MORALITY, which is comprised in seventy duodecimo pages.

THIS CERTIFIES THAT MASTER

for his regular deportment at the academy, and for the progress, which he has made, in those branches to which he has attended, is entitled to the commendation of his friends and instructer.

TIMOTHY ALDEN, JUN. PRECEPTOR.

DEMARARA-STREET, PORTSMOUTH, NEWHAMPSHIRE, XIII JANUARY, MDCCCVII.

Catalog of pupils for Reverend Timothy Alden's Academy for the quarter ending January 1807. Collections of Portsmouth Athenaeum. Dan Gair photograph.

By 1799, Timothy Alden had arrived in Portsmouth to take up his post as Collegiate Pastor of South Church and as educator. He soon opened the doors of his Young Ladies Academy and within a few years the surnames of the most prominent Portsmouth families appeared on its rosters of students.

While history may have treated the Rev. Alden unkindly with respect to his oratory skills, he no doubt made a profound impression on those who, in 1801, heard his Century Sermon, "The Glory of America." Alden was a superlative educator with a strong sense of purpose—that his students be provided with a quality education. "The object of this institution," Alden advertised in 1801, "is to teach both sexes in the various branches which are usually taught at the most noted academies in the United States so that the Masters may have opportunity to prepare for the tutoring room or for college and the misses for acquiring each an education, so as to preclude the necessity of going ahead for that purpose."[19]

It is from Rev. Alden's academy that we are first able to document specific needleworks with a particular school. Certificates of achievement like that issued to John Greenleaf, a student in the Second Class of Masters in 1806, reveal the variety of types of needlework taught at the academy. Here students are identified as having done embroidery, painting, and needlework pictures—described by Alden simply as "pieces of embroidery."[20]

Among his first class of scholars in 1801 was thirteen-year-old Catherine Whipple Langdon, daughter of Woodbury and Sarah Sherburne Langdon of Portsmouth. Two years later she recorded the events of her day in her journal:

> I spend the remainder of the forenoon with my needle. [We] go in afternoon to a female society. This society is established by 11 young ladies formerly under the tuition of the Rev. Mr. Alden, united by bonds of friend-ship. I attended with the rest of Mr. Alden's scholars the funeral of Miss Deborah Leighton. She was a scholar of Mr. Alden.[21]

The distinctive samplers stitched by Sally Blunt and Mary Ann Hooker were most probably made at Rev. Alden's academy in 1804 and 1805, respectively. Both girls are known to have attended classes here. The samplers, worked on green linsey-woolsey grounds, share nearly identical borders, matching alphabets with numerals 1 through

*1827 catalog of the first female school in Portsmouth, New Hampshire. Portsmouth Athenaeum collections.*

12 alternating with a cross-stitched *X* punctuated by a dot. Each girl used the same basket motif and verse, "How blest the maid whom circling years improve." In addition, identical crossband designs separate the lower and upper portions of the samplers and the girls' names and ages are each enclosed within a scallop shell. Mary Ann added the year under her name and Sally placed an NH at the base of her shell, possibly intending to inscribe it with the place-name, Portsmouth.

A mourning scene worked by Lydia Gerrish was stitched at the academy in 1806 and recorded for history on the certificate issued to John Greenleaf.

From about 1801 until 1805, Alden divided his duties between those of his pastorate and those as chief educator at his academy on Demarara Street. However, in 1805 the financial strain seems to have forced Alden into making a choice between his pastoral mission and that of educator. He petitioned the proprietors of South Parish: "I am unwilling to spend any more of my time in a twofold employment, when the duties of the pastoral office alone are sufficient to engross every faculty of the greatest genius," he wrote in April of that year.[22]

In June, Alden responded to an inquiry from the South Parish proprietors as to what "conditions he would consent to continue [as] their Gospel Minister" with a request for additional wages, "twenty cords of hardwood annually, a parsonage equal to the one occupied by the Rev. Buckminster, and an outright grant of $500."[23] With this, the ties that bound unraveled and for the next three years Alden devoted himself entirely to running his academy and to writing. The effort, though, was not enough to sustain him financially, and early in 1808 he closed the doors of the academy for the last time.

Though Timothy Alden died in relative obscurity in Pennsylvania in 1839, he had made an impact on a number of important American institutions. After leaving Portsmouth he assisted in the organization of the American Antiquarian Society, was librarian of the Massachusetts and the New York Historical Societies, headed the Newark Academy in Newark, New Jersey, and founded Allegheny College in Meadville, Pennsylvania. Each of these institutions continues in operation today.

Families of means sometimes looked outside Portsmouth for a school for their daughters. The reputation of a much revered teacher prompted some Portsmouth and Kittery families to send their children to the Mrs. Saunder's and Miss Beach's Academy, Clifton Hill, in Dorchester, Massachusetts. The roster of students included Ann Elizabeth Salter, who married the grandson of Stephen Chase, Christopher Toppan. Also attending Clifton Hill at various times were Sarah Larkin, Sarah Chauncy Cutts, Sarah Ann, and Maria Rice, and Ann Rindge Pierce.[24] Between 1804 and 1829 Portsmouth daughters also attended Misses Martin's School in Portland, Maine. They included Betsey and Harriet Clark, Lucy Maria and Eliza Goddard, Abigail Ham, Mary Harris, and Jane Mackay.[25]

Seven known samplers that are similar in design and reflect a common influence of the schoolmasters were probably worked under the tutelage of Miss Elizabeth Ward. Mary Langdon's (1800) sampler shares similarities with those of Henrietta Tuttell (1803), Abigail Bowles (1804), Martha Gaines (1804), Sarah Catherine Moffatt Odiorne (1806), Mary Gerrish (1811), and Mary Elizabeth Coffin (1814).

On April 28, 1818, a student in the school operated by Elizabeth S. Smith completed the first known "Portsmouth" sampler. She was Priscilla Hall Badger, the daughter of a stone and tinware dealer in Portsmouth, John Badger. Although no advertisements have been found for their school, it appears that Elizabeth Smith, along with her sister Mary Ann, had established a school for young misses in their father's house on Vaughan Street in Portsmouth. Nearly ten years later, in 1827, Elizabeth is identified as an instructress at an academy on Daniel Street.[26]

Some six months later, two more samplers depicting the now familiar scene of a house, fence, trees with birds, and a barn with a nearby birdhouse were completed within thirteen days of each other. Deborah Laighton, under the tutelage of Mary Ann Smith, completed her sampler on October 15, 1818; and on October 28, 1818, Caroline Vaughan, a student of Mary Walden, completed hers.

Earlier in 1818, Mary Walden placed an advertisement in the *Portsmouth Oracle* announcing the "Spring Quarter of her Drawing School the first Monday in May." Her school was in her father's house on Penhallow Street, only two blocks from the Smith sisters' school.[27] As was the case with Elizabeth Smith, Mary Walden had the help of her sister, Elvira Walden.

The four teachers were close in age and lived near one another. During the years when they would themselves have been students, about 1808 to 1811, several teachers offered instruction in needlework. But only George Dame, advertising in 1808, offered to teach his students the art of "designating patterns for the use of the needle."[28] Dame's classes were held in the Assembly Hall, on the corner of Vaughan Street and Raitts Court, not far from the girls' homes. "DRAWING & PAINTING furnish a pleasing amusement," he wrote in his advertisement of March 29, "and are necessary accomplishments for your ladies...in the display of taste and genius on paper, silk, etc. etc."

George Dame and his school enjoyed great favor in Portsmouth and it is likely that the two pairs of sisters were in his classroom in the Assembly Hall. Dame is also the only teacher of the period to emphasize the drawing of patterns for various purposes including needlework. Indeed, it may well have been in Dame's school that at least one of the girls was inspired to create the now familiar

Portsmouth pattern for samplers.

From here the pattern must have been brought into the repertoire of their own schools and became popular among their students. Succeeding generations of students, having seen the pattern worked by their friends, continued the tradition of re-creating the scene until at least 1840. So far we have identified nearly thirty "Portsmouth" samplers.

Others advertising at the same time as Dame include Serena Parker Johnson and Fanny Dow in 1808–09 and Mary E. Hill in 1810. Charles Taft, advertising from 1808 to 1811, operated his school as an extension of the academy begun by the Rev. Timothy Alden. Taft informed his readers that his

**George Dame,**

RESPECTFULLY informs his friends and the public in general of his late return to Portsmouth; and that he has taken a room in Mr *Nathaniel B March's* building, directly opposite Mr *C Peirce's* Bookstore in Daniel street, with an intention of continuing the

**Painting Business,**

in its various branches; and flatters himself from the liberal encouragement and constant practice he has had of late years, to be enabled to execute his work in a style worthy the attention of those why may wish to possess likenesses of their friends. His price is fifteen dollars each, but should he fail to take a likeness to their satisfaction no gratuity will be expected. Price of Portrait Painting from 10 to 25 dollars each.

Mr. D. also solicits encouragement in other branches of Painting, Gilding, &c. on Signs, Window and Bed Cornices, Dressing Tables, Wash Stand, Chairs, Fire Buckets, &c — Gilding and Ornamental Work on Glass for Looking Glasses, Pictures, Shop Signs, &c.

Standards and Drums painted in the neatest manner—Drawing and Painting on Silk for Embroidery—Patterns for Ladies Needle Work, &c. &c—all of which he will engage to do on the most reasonable terms and short notice —           *September* 17

*Advertisement placed by George Dame for his school in the September 17, 1811, issue of the* New Hampshire Gazette.

school "commenced in the same rooms occupied by the Rev. Alden, for the same purpose, to teach plain and fine needlework."

Each of the samplers worked in 1818 was rendered on a green linsey-woolsey ground. In time this would become another "signature" of Portsmouth samplers. Many variations of the Portsmouth sampler emerged, and not all were worked on linsey-woolsey. Indeed, many were worked—like the one made by Mary Ellen Cleaves in 1832—on unbleached linen. Still, the Cleaves sampler retains the familiar design motif incorporating a two-story house with a fence, birdhouse, barn, and three to five trees with perching birds.

Other distinguishing elements of Portsmouth samplers that are constant over a period of time include the cherubs found in eight samplers, those worked by Caroline Vaughan in 1818, Deborah Laighton in 1819, Adaline M. Ferguson in 1822, Ann Elizabeth Ham in 1826, Emily Furber in 1827, Frances M. Tuckerman in 1829, Martha Jane Fowler in 1835, and Sarah Emily Currier in 1840.

A geometrically shaped basket with identically fashioned handles and flower blossoms that are strongly similar in design and placement can be seen in the samplers worked by Emily Furber in 1827, Elizabeth Fabian Willey in 1834, and Sarah Emily Currier in 1840.

The samplers worked by Furber, Willey, and Tuckerman all share identically shaped smaller baskets of flowers with identical groupings of blossoms.

The sampler worked by Harriet Ann Dockum and signed in Portsmouth in 1825 includes the familiar scene along with trees worked in a highly geometric and stylized fashion identical to the trees found on the Portsmouth samplers worked by Ann M. Gerrish in 1832 and Elizabeth Fabyan Willey in 1834. In 1826 Ann Elizabeth Ham also included trees worked in a geometric fashion in her sampler, rendering them in a pyramid style.

Geometrically shaped baskets with brightly colored round fruit mounded in a pyramid are another element shared by a number of Portsmouth samplers. They include those worked by Lucy Maria Wiggin in 1822, Harriet Ann Dockum in 1825, Ann Elizabeth Ham in 1826, Ann Mary Gerrish in 1832, and Sarah E. Gerrish in 1839. In 1832 Sarah Elizabeth Marden included footed compote dishes, similarly mounded with fruit, in her sampler.

While each of these elements categorizes certain of the Portsmouth samplers, these same elements also span the entire field of samplers that survive from the period. Rather than isolating groups of samplers, these motifs link the works from student to student and classroom to classroom for some one hundred years.

Certainly there had been a wide variety of forms of needlework taught in Portsmouth over the course of this period. Advertisements included offers of instruction in the making of crewelwork pocketbooks in Irish stitch, the drawing and working of "twilight," marking of letters, plain sewing, working samplers and pictures. Instruction in the working of coats of arms, print work, and "Dresden" also were offered.

During the Federal period, there was an increased emphasis on

drawing and a new attention to painting of silk, wood, paper, and velvet, along with frequent offers of instruction in tambouring.

Some four years after George Dame advertised instruction in
the "designating" of patterns, a Mrs. Wyatt advertised that she had
just "obtained some new and fashionable patterns for mourning pieces,
either to be painted or embroidered." These were prints that could be
copied and interpreted in needlework pictures and mourning scenes.

The most fascinating account of school life in early-nineteenth-
century Portsmouth was penned in about 1876 by Sarah Parker Rice
Goodwin, in her journal. Sarah, who was born in Portsmouth in 1802,
recollects having attended at least nine schools by the time she was
fifteen years old. Her remembrances are both pointed—she believed in
speaking her mind—and amusing. What is more, she writes of some of
the teachers whose names appear in these pages, along with some
who remain unknown to us except for their mention in her journal.
While many objects owned by Sarah and her husband, Ichabod, have
survived, examples of her needlework do not seem to be among them.

The elderly Sarah treats us to a candid review of the tenor of
education in general among Portsmouth's early teachers, reminding
us that what we have found in records and surviving needleworks is
representative of a much broader scenario. Sitting comfortably in her
home on then fashionable Islington Street (the house was moved to
Strawbery Banke Museum), she wrote:

> My first school was under Marm Plaisted. She sat in the mid-
> dle of the room in an arm chair, her husbands big cane resting
> against it. About twenty children usually attended and they
> were all very much afraid of her cane. She had sharp black
> eyes and wore large round spectacles and a mop cap. When she
> dismissed school she would say, "Elizabeth Ham, curtsey and
> go; Sarah Rice, curtsey and go; Daniel Ham, bow and go; John
> Boardman, bow and go." and so on ...
>
> Then I went to a Mrs. Williams on Mark Lane and there
> I accomplished my first triumph in linen shirt making. ... Then
> I was sent to Mrs. John Briard, an Irish woman of some educa-
> tion and devoted to making pillow lace and purling, I don't
> think I learned anything there. After that I went to a Miss
> Richards. ... We had good times there and there was a show of
> learning.
>
> Then I went to the Academy which at that time had a

full board of trustees with Preceptor and Preceptress. I was in the fifth class with five or six girls about my own age, but the preceptress was bordering on insanity and very melancholy and kept me in strokes a whole year and often carried me to her boarding house as a punishment for not getting my lessons. ... Well, poor soul, in one year she was sent to some asylum and I was relieved. Then I was sent to Mr. Blake and Mrs. Olney. Such a pretender as she was! It was all prayers, bible readings, tears and nonsense. ... After that Mr. Austin and his sister, Miss Sarah, opened a rare seminary for young ladies and gentlemen. I learned all I wanted to there and for three years had a grand good time.

By this time I was fifteen years old and as Miss Willard's school of young ladies was in great repute, I went there. ... I think it was the most perfect school I have ever known anything about. Everybody learned, or almost everybody; everybody was happy and revered and loved the teacher.[29]

Sarah's odyssey through the schoolrooms of Portsmouth probably began when she was about five and ended when she was eighteen. And if Timothy Alden's offer to provide an education for children that would "preclude the necessity of going ahead for that purpose" at first seems cryptic to us, then Sarah has helped make it clear. There were numerous schools of dubious reputation from which to choose. No doubt that is true of instruction in needlework as well. We all too often blame the needleworker for poor work rather than the teacher. To bend the twig, so lyrically proposed by Alexander Pope in 1735, is no simple matter after all.

# Chronology of Sampler and Needlework Teachers in Portsmouth, New Hampshire, 1765–1840

1765 **Widow Winkley**
*New Hampshire Gazette,* July 5
"Boarding and Schooling for Young Ladies"

1770 **Ruth Jones**
*New Hampshire Gazette,* February 16
"… all the various Arts and Branches of Needlework on Lawn, Flowering with Cruel Working Pocket Books with Irish Stitch, drawing and working of Twilights, Marking of letters, and Plain Sewing"

1772 **Mary Homans**
*New Hampshire Gazette,* March 20
"… any Sort of NeedleWork"

1774 **Sarah Winkley and Elizabeth Hill**
*New Hampshire Gazette,* May 24
"… all sorts of Work, in the neatest and best manner, viz. Working Samplers, Pictures, Coat of Arms"

1780– **Benjamin Dearborn**
1791 *New Hampshire Gazette,* April 30, 1791
"Embroidery, plain Needlework"

*Reward of Merit issued to Charlotte Ladd by her instructress, Rebecca Hardy. Collections of Portsmouth Athenaeum. Dan Gair photograph.*

**1784   Mrs. Montague**
*Brewster's Rambles* (p. 303) and *Portsmouth Historic and Picturesque* (p. 304)
"... preceptress of first public school for female instruction in Portsmouth"

**1786   Mrs. Warnwell**
*New Hampshire Gazette,* May 3
"... will open a genteel Boarding School for the reception of Young Ladies, who will be taught everything necessary to complete their education"

**1791   Mrs. Spillard with Rev. Ogden**
*The Spy,* August 6, 10, 13, 17, 20
"... she instructs in reading and the various useful and ornamental branches of needle-work. Her residence and school are now in the hands of Rev. Mr. Ogden"

**1791–  Samuel Tappan with Amos Tappan**
1802    *New Hampshire Gazette,* Feb. 26, 1791, March 27, 1796
        *Portsmouth Chronicle,* March 27, 1802
        "… a lady will be employed to instruct the Misses in Needle-Work"
        (See also Rockingham County, New Hampshire Probate records #10325 OS.)

**1800    Miss Guy**
        *New Hampshire Gazette,* April 9
        "… for instructing Embroidery, Plain Needlework"

**1800–  Rev. Timothy Alden, Miss Margaret Cushing, Miss**
**1808    Elizabeth Allen, Miss Sarah Cogswell**
        *Portsmouth Oracle,* March 13
        "… common needlework … the ornamental branches of needle-work"

**1802–  Mrs. Mary Hart**
1808    *Portsmouth Oracle,* March 13.
        "… common needlework … the ornamental branches of needle-work"

**1803    Thomas Jackson**
        *U.S. Oracle & Advertiser,* July 9.

**1804–  Miss Barrell**
1816    *Portsmouth Oracle,* August 3
        "The children will be instructed in Reading, English Grammar, Spelling, Plain & Ornamental Needle Work"

        *Portsmouth Oracle,* March 29
        "Plain Sewing, Embroidery, Print Work, and Dresden"

        *Portsmouth Journal,* March 26
        "The branches which will be attended to are Plain Sewing, Reading, Spelling, English Grammar, Embroidery, Printwork and Dresden"

> # *FEMALE ACADEMY.*
> THE LADIES of PORTSMOUTH and its vicinity, are informed that a FE- MALE ACADEMY will be opened on the 19th September, by
> ## *Mrs. MARY HART.*
> The branches which will be particularly attended to, are Reading, Writing, Arithmetic, and Geography, plain and ornamental Needle work.
>
> Those LADIES who wish to place their children under her tuition, are requested to make early application for that purpose.
>
> ☞ A few MISSES may be accomodated with Board. *Portsmouth, August 9.*

*Advertisement by Mary Hart for her school that ran in the* New Hampshire Gazette *in 1803.*

*New Hampshire Gazette,* April 2
"Miss Barrel has Taken a room in The Museum"

1805 **Miss Briant**
*Portsmouth Oracle,* July 27
"School for Young Misses at a room on Spring Hill. Drawing, embroidery, working muslin, marking, plain sewing, Reading, Writing, Arithmetic, English and Grammar."

1806 **Miss Ward**
Bolton and Coe, *American Samplers,* p. 382.
Sampler worked by Sarah Catherine Moffatt Odiorne under her tutelage. (See Rockingham County New Hampshire Probate records #14631 OS.)

**1808–  George Dame**
1812  *New Hampshire
Gazette,* April 19
"Drawing and Paint-
ing furnish a pleas-
ing ornament ... not
only in the display of
taste and genius, on
paper, silks, etc. but
in drawing and des-
ignating patterns"

*New Hampshire
Gazette,* March 29
"Young Ladies'
Academy, Drawing &
Painting designating
patterns for use of
the needle"

## Mr. Charles Taft.

HAVING commenced his Academy for the instruction of Young Ladies, at that commodious room recently occupied by the Rev'd Mr. Alden, informs the inhabitants of Portfmouth and its vicinity, that he still continues to receive Pupils for the several branches of Education, viz *Orthography, Reading, Writing, Arithmetic, English Grammar, Compofition, &c. &c.* Those Parents, who would avail themfelves of the prefent opportunity, will pleafe to make early application.

The Preceptor flatters himfelf, that by his unremitting endeavours to imprefs on the minds of his Pupils, not only the principles and ufe of fcience, but thofe of morality and virtue, he shall meet the approbation and acceptance of his generous Patrons.
Portfmouth, April 19, 1808.

### TAKE NOTICE.

**1808  Thomas Jackson**
*New Hampshire
Gazette,* March 22
"The Subscriber has
it in contemplation
to procure a Lady
capable of instruct-
ing Young Ladies in
all the branches of useful and ornamental Needle Work and
Painting, etc."

*Advertisement for a school run by Charles Taft
that was placed in the April 19, 1808, issue of
the* New Hampshire Gazette.

**1808  Mrs. Part**
*New Hampshire Gazette,* March 22
"Embroidery, Plain and fancy needle works"

**1808–  Serena Parker Johnson**
1809  *Portsmouth Journal,* April l, 1809
"... useful and ornamental branches of Needlework. Terms for
those who attend to English Grammar and ornamental Needlework 3 dollars 50 cents"

**1808– Charles Taft**
1811 *Portsmouth Journal,* April 2
"… plain and fine Needlework"

**1809 Fanny Dow**
*New Hampshire Gazette,* March 28
"… she will teach useful Needlework"

**1810 Mary E. Hill**
Bolton and Coe, *American Samplers*, p. 382.
Sampler worked by Sarah Fitzgerald

*Portsmouth Oracle,* Oct. 12, 1816
Death Notice, age 31

**1811 S. Hayes**
*New Hampshire Gazette,* April 2
"Drawing, Painting and Embroidery"

**1812 Eliza H. C. Hilton**
*New Hampshire Gazette,* March 10
"Ornamental branches of needle-work"

**1812 Mrs. Wyatt**
*New Hampshire Gazette,* March 10
"Painting in water colors, on paper, satin, cambric and wood
together with various kinds of fancy work. Mrs. W. obtained
some new and fashionable patterns for mourning pieces, either
to be painted or embroidered"

**1814– Mary Ann Weare Swett**
1822 *New Hampshire Gazette,* Nov. 21
Kenney "intends opening a School, in an apartment of her
father's house in Mendum Street"

*Portsmouth Oracle,* Sept. 27, 1817
Announcement that "the Exhibition of her scholars will commence next Thursday Evening, at half past six o'clock"

*New Hampshire Gazette,* March 5 and 19, 1822
"Widow Mary Ann Kenney Respectfully informs the citizens of
Portsmouth and the vicinity, that her School for the instruction
of Children and Youth of Both sexes will ... pay the strictest
attention to their department and instruct them in Orthography, Reading, Writing, English Grammar, Arithmetic, plain
and Ornamental Needlework. Formerly Mary Ann Weare,
lately M. A. Swett, now as above"

1816 **Sarah Hart**
*Portsmouth Oracle,* March 9
"...her school will commence the 1st day of April"

1816 **Sarah P. Horney**
*Portsmouth Oracle,* Feb. 24
"School for the Instruction of Young Ladies"
(See Sarah in section on students; also see appendix.)

1816 **Eliza Ann Toppan**
*Portsmouth Oracle,* Feb. 10
"... with all kinds of Needlework"

1816 **A. J. Richards**
*Portsmouth Oracle,* March 2
"Embroidery, Tambouring, Cotton and plain Work, &c"

1816– **Mrs. C. Clark**
1817 *Portsmouth Oracle,* March 23
"... will be open for the reception of Young Ladies and Children"

*Portsmouth Oracle,* April 5, 1817
"... will resume her School on Tuesday 1st of April"

1816– **Mr. and Mrs. Hart**
1818 *Portsmouth Oracle,* Feb. 17
"Plain Sewing, Marking, Working Muslin, Tambouring, Print
Work on Satin, Drawing and Painting on silk, wood & paper"

1817 **Miss Payson**
*Portsmouth Oracle,* March 22
"Academy will open to Young Ladies"

**1817 Sarah Whittier**
*New Hampshire Gazette,* March 11
*Portsmouth Oracle,* March 13
"Plain Sewing, working on cambric and muslins, tambouring, drawing, painting on paper, wood, silk and velvet together with embroidering on silk and velvet"

**1817 Miss Eustis**
*Portsmouth Oracle,* April 5
"… will resume her School on Tuesday 1st of April."

**1817 Miss Haven**
*New Hampshire Gazette,* April 1

**1817– Sarah W. Austin and Daniel Austin**
**1821** *New Hampshire Gazette,* Dec. 27
*Portsmouth Oracle,* Dec. 27
"… with the assistance of his Sister, Sarah W. Austin, Plain Sewing, Marking, Drawing, Painting, Print work on silk, Tambouring, Working Muslin, Embroidery"

**1818 E. D. Hall**
*New Hampshire Gazette,* Feb. 24
"Miss E. D. Hall informs her friends that her School is open for the reception of Misses, at her Fathers House, in Deer Street"

**1818– Mary Walden and Elvira Walden**
**1822** *Portsmouth Oracle,* March 24
"Miss Walden will commence the Spring Quarter of her Drawing School the first Monday in May."
Sampler worked by Caroline Vaughan under Mary Walden.
Sampler worked by Adeline M. Ferguson under Elvira Walden.

**1818– Elizabeth S. Smith and Mary Ann Smith**
**1822** Sampler worked by Priscilla Hall Badger under Elizabeth S. Smith.
Sampler worked by Deborah Laighton under Mary Ann Smith.
*Portsmouth City Directory 1821*
*Portsmouth City Directory 1827:* Removal—Elizabeth Smith, Instructress of Academy, Daniel Street.

1819    **Samuel Bowles**
        *New Hampshire Gazette,* March 13
        "... all kinds of Needlework, plain and ornamental"
        (See Rockingham County, New Hampshire, Probate records
        #14045.)

1821    **Misses Austin**
        *New Hampshire Gazette,* March 20

1821    **Misses Bagley**
        *New Hampshire Gazette,* Nov 26

1821–   **Eliza Sullivan**
1822    *Portsmouth Journal,* Oct. 6
        "Ornamental Needle Work on very reasonable terms"

1822    **Miss Spoffard with Miss Smith**
        *New Hampshire Gazette,* March 19
        "Drawing and projection of maps, Painting, Ornamental
        Needlework"

1823    **Martha W. Hill and Mary M. Hill**
        *Portsmouth Journal,* March 29
        "... intend opening a school for the instruction of MISSES"

1823    **Miss R. Hardy**
        *Portsmouth Journal,* March 28
        "... instruction of Young Ladies in the useful and ornamental
        branches of Education"
        (See Rockingham County Probate records #18936 OS.)

1824    **Miss Folsom's Academy**
        Certificate to Charlotte Ladd at Miss Folsom's Academy
        (Coues Family Papers. Scrapbook. 1835–1867. Ms. 11
        Portsmouth Athenaeum, Portsmouth, New Hampshire)

1826    **Mr. A. B. Engstrom**
        *New Hampshire Gazette,* Dec. 5
        "Mr. A. B. Engstrom would inform the inhabitants of
        Portsmouth that mourning pieces and perspective painting will
        be taught in his school in Daniel Street"

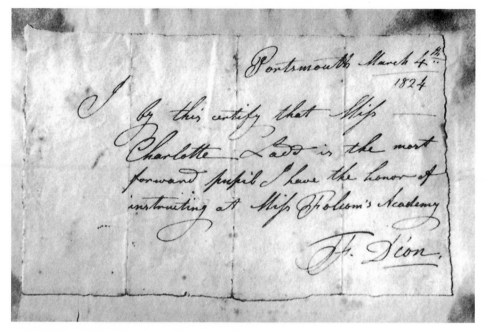

*Certificate of Award issued to Charlotte Ladd as the most forward pupil at Miss Folsom's Academy in 1824. Collections of the Portsmouth Athenaeum. Dan Gair photograph.*

1826   **Sarah W. Austin**
*Portsmouth Journal,* May 20
"Miss Sarah W. Austin has commenced instruction in Drawing and Painting in Water Colours, and Drawing in Crayons, with the addition of ornamental needlework at the School House in Parker's Lane"

1826   **Ann L. C. Jones**
Sampler worked by Ann Elizabeth Ham

1826   **Suzannah Appleton**
Portsmouth School Report for 1826 indicating needlework taught, 57 students; Pitt Street

1826   **Caroline Sewell**
Portsmouth School Report for 1826 indicating needlework taught, 53 students; Gates Street

1827    **Mary Vaughan**
Portsmouth Female Asylum
*Portsmouth City Directory 1827*
Instruction in needlework a required subject

1828    **Mary Ann Furnald Hall**
Sampler worked by Mary Ann Marden
*Portsmouth City Directory 1834*
"Miss Hall, opposite E. Wentworth's, Pleasant Street"

1829    **Miss L. E. Penhallow**
*New Hampshire Gazette,* March 3
"Will open a school for the instruction of young ladies"

1829    **E. Robinson**
Sampler worked by Frances Whidden
Strawbery Banke Museum

1829    **Miss C. Sherburne**
*Portsmouth Journal & Rockingham Gazette,* April 4
"Also, Lace Work, Muslin, Embroidery, and particular attention
to plain Sewing. Terms $2 and $3"

1830    **F. D. S. Sherburne**
*Portsmouth Journal & Rockingham Gazette,* April 10.
"Miss F. D. S. Sherburne would like to give lessons in Dress
Cutting and in Embroidery. Any branch of needlework done at
the same place"

1831–   **Miss Spalding**
1834    *Portsmouth Journal & Rockingham Gazette,* March 12
*Portsmouth City Directory 1834*
"School for Young Ladies"

1832    **Mary Ann Whidden**
Sampler worked by Sarah Elizabeth Marden

1834    **Eliza Jane Bennett**
Catalog and Synopsis of the First Female School in
Portsmouth, New Hampshire, March 1, 1827
*Portsmouth City Directory 1834*

1834   **Lucy M. Wiggin, Caroline E. Foss, Lavinia H. Young**
       *Portsmouth City Directory 1834*
       "The schools taught by Lucy M. Wiggin, Caroline E. Foss and
       Lavinia H. Young are taught by Masters in the winter and by
       Misses in the summer"

1834   Female Private Schools
       *Portsmouth City Directory*
       **Miss E. C. and Caroline Langdon**
       Upper Academy Hall
       **Miss Elizabeth Spalding**
       Lower Academy Hall
       **Miss Mary Cooper and Miss Mary Palmer**
       Juvenile Study, Broad Street
       **Mrs. Gotham**
       State Street
       **Miss Bagley**
       Pitt Street
       **Misses Lucretia A. Lyman & Miss Elizabeth Lunt**
       State Street
       **Misses Salter**
       Livermore Street
       **Miss Rebecca Hardy**
       Corner of Cross and High Streets
       **Misses Melcher**
       Broad Street
       **Miss Yeaton**
       Daniel Street
       **Miss Hall**
       Opposite E. Wentworth's, Pleasant Street
       **Miss Mary Blaisdell**
       Pitt Street
       **Miss Lucinda Holman**
       Jackson Street
       **Miss Jane Winkley**
       High Street
       **Miss Ann Southerin**
       Opposite Robinson's Hotel, Congress Street
       **Miss Tisdale**
       Russell Street

**Miss Hardy**
Parkers Lane
**Miss Melcher**
Corner Akerman and Rundlet Streets
**Miss Susan P. Dennett**
North Street

1835    **Mrs. Ann L Marshall**
Silver medal awarded to Caroline Huntress for excellence in
sewing, reading and writing in 1835
This award was presented to the Portsmouth Historical Society, Portsmouth, New Hampshire

1839    Female Private Schools
*Portsmouth City Directory*
**Miss Sarah C. Badger**
5 Manning Street
**Miss Sarah H. Bagley**
38 Daniel Street
**Miss Mary Blaisdell**
44 Court Street corner of Atkinson Street
**Miss Susannah Clark**
31 Daniel Street
**Miss Eliza Clark & Miss Frances M. Day**
92 State Street corner of Chestnut Street
**Miss Hannah Cutter & Miss Helen C. Cross**
Academy, entrance 1 Middle Street
**Mrs. Charles Gotham**
48 State Street
**Miss Ann Emily Ham**
17 Islington Street
**Miss Elizabeth C. Ham**
2 Dennett Street
**Miss Mary Hayes**
34 Deer Street
**Mrs. Thomas Hoyt**
5 Hancock Street
**Miss Sophia Johnson**
26 Hanover Street
**Mrs. Catharine Melcher**
81 State Street

**Miss Harriet N. Moulton**
92 State Street corner of Chestnut Street
**Miss Abigail Salter**
53 Pleasant Street
**Miss Eliza Salter**
53 Pleasant Street
**Miss Sarah E. Salter**
27 State Street
**Mrs. Eliza Ann Tripe**
90 State Street
**Misses Lucy Maria and Harriet Walker**
2 Russell Street, corner of Vaughan Street
**Mrs. Jane S. Winkley**
19 High Street

# The Sampler and Needlework Students in Portsmouth, New Hampshire, 1741–1840

*Females attend, and hear a friend*
*Unfold strange things to view—*
*Now to be wife and make good wives—*
*The things you ought to do.*[30]

WHEN THIS POEM was published in the *New Hampshire Gazette* in 1790, the "things you ought to do" included taking instruction in elocution, grammar, vocabulary, geography, and mathematics. And although there was no mention of the ornamental and useful arts, provisions for teaching young ladies the use of the embroidery and darning needles held just as much sway among Portsmouth's gentry as they did elsewhere in America at the time. Newspaper advertisements for female schools including some instruction in needlework far outnumbered those without, indicating that needlework occupied a vital spot in a young lady's course of education.

Portsmouth needlework students of the eighteenth and early nineteenth centuries, here represented by the work that survives them, were the daughters of sea captains and shipbuilders; of merchants, politicians, and successful public officials; of gentlemen farmers and prosperous artisan-businessmen. The now legendary surnames of Portsmouth history, those of Langdon, Cutts, Peirce, Blunt, Wentworth, Haven, Sherburne, and Melcher, among many others, are liberally sprinkled throughout accounts and records of Portsmouth female educational institutions during this period.

As beneficiaries of the new "ideal" education, so enthusiastically received by teachers, parents, and students alike, it was only natural that many of the young women would want to share with those less fortunate. They would, after all, be helping other women to become more valuable wives and citizens.

The founding of the Portsmouth Female Asylum in 1804 was underwritten by the work of some one hundred fifty "liberal females."[31] "In the Female Asylum," wrote the author of an early accounting of the school, "the children are taught to read and sew; they are instructed in the principles of religion; their habits are subjected to a salutary discipline; and particular attention is paid to their neatness and personal cleanliness."

The mission of the asylum was to "rescue" orphaned females and in so doing turn them away from a life of "the accumulated misery of poverty and vice," toward one as a wife and mother where she would "increase the virtue of the circle in which she moves, and ... communicate the blessing to other children and other families." While the institution eventually stopped operating, it is interesting to note that funds invested at its closing were being used in the 1870s and '80s to pay the wages of sewing teachers in the public school system.

Lucy Maria Wiggin, whose "Portsmouth" sampler is in the collections of Strawbery Banke, was a typical student of the early nineteenth century in that she was the daughter of a well-to-do farmer, passed her education on by teaching summer classes in the 1834 Female Public School, and married into economic circumstances similar to those from which she had come.

Others used this skill and knowledge to support themselves as teachers. Lydia Peirce, for instance, was engaged by Mrs. Mary Chase, wife of the wealthy merchant Stephen Chase—whose house is now part of the Strawbery Banke Museum—to give instruction to her two grandchildren, Mary Tappan and Harriet Crosby, as we know from the receipt signed by Lydia in the summer of 1809.[32] It is likely that she spent some time supervising the girls in a needlework project. Mr. Chase's daughter-in-law, Sally Blunt, whose sampler is also discussed here and was most probably done at Rev. Alden's academy, taught in the South Parish Sunday School until September 1824, when she entered into "domestic arrangements," having accepted William Chase's hand in marriage.[33]

The most thorough detailing of a Portsmouth child's education in the early part of the nineteenth century can be found in the rare survival of the accounting of a guardianship to a Court of Probate. In

1806, Gilbert Horney of Portsmouth died, leaving his neighbor and friend, the silversmith William Simes, guardian of his young daughter, Sarah.[34]

From July 1806 until September 1815, Simes attended to his duties as guardian keeping careful records of his expenditures, which he in turn submitted to the court. Today the document allows us a glimpse into how this young lady's life was managed for her over the course of some nine years (see Appendix).

During this period Simes provided for her boarding, initially with her mother or grandmother and then later in the boardinghouse of Miss Sarah Purcell, now known as the John Paul Jones House. He also saw to it that she was provided with clothing, and paid bills to such men as merchant Samuel Larkin for books and for her schooling to George Dame, Mrs. Hart, and to a J. Hart. Instruction in needlework was included; payments for articles such as silk, scissors, cambric, a paint box, thimbles, and knitting "pins" coincide with payments for schooling. Unfortunately, there is no example of her work for us to see today. One would like to think that perhaps Sarah would have wanted it that way. Not every young lady managed to cultivate a fondness for the needle and thread.

The supplies that Sarah Horney purchased could be found in any of a number of dry goods shops in Portsmouth, such as the shop kept at the foot of State Street by Stephen Chase. The 1805 inventory of his stock included over twelve hundred yards of fabric as well as needles, thimbles, thread, marking canvas, pins, buttons, and "elastic." Elastic, according to Dobson's Encyclopedia—the authority of the day, having begun publication in America in 1798—was used "by painters for rubbing out black-lead pencil marks."

In 1816 the Misses M. and E. Wentworth advertised some of the latest arrivals of "new Goods." They included marking canvas, silk, and cotton floss, sewing silk, cotton sewing thread, and black and white cambric. Mrs. Wyatt, who was teaching in 1812, also advertised that she had "obtained some new and fashionable patterns for mourning pieces."[35]

The advertisements placed by teachers in Portsmouth between about 1765 and 1840 attest to the wide variety of instruction to be had here. Like changes in fashion, new needlework artforms found popularity among the young scholars and their teachers, who were eager to keep pace and to swell the ranks with new students. As the years passed, needlework, which included crewel, the working of samplers, print work, and Dresden, in part gave way to the latest vogue for needlework pictures, tambourwork, drawing, and painting on silk, paper, and velvet, and for the working of mourning scenes. Plain sewing remained in the curriculum late into the nineteenth century and could still be found on the list of subjects taught in numerous schools even after the turn of the century.

All the while, changes in popular taste in Portsmouth kept up with what was happening in other cities and towns along the eastern seaboard. Mourning scenes, for instance, had become all the rage by the start of the nineteenth century. Teachers tried to keep the concept fresh by offering new "patterns" or pictures to be copied whenever they could. The working of silk embroidered pictures had gained such a foothold that in 1807 the Rev. Timothy Alden not only listed those students working needlework pictures or mourning scenes on the certificates of attendance he issued, but he also identified the picture each girl had completed by its familiar title. Clearly, the themes of these pictures were widely known. They included Flora, the Roman goddess of flowers; Melpomene, the Greek goddess of tragedy; mourning scenes; landscapes; and children being instructed in geography.

As the mid-nineteenth century approached, fewer and fewer silk pictures, especially mourning scenes, were being worked. Mourning scenes and family genealogies, once worked entirely with the needle, were reduced to painted preprinted paper versions. Samplers, on the other hand—sometimes worked with very elaborate decorative motifs—continued to be made here until at least 1840.

That work of such high caliber could still be found here as late as 1840 testifies in part to the value placed on such objects by their makers. In some instances, samplers worked by mothers and their daughters have survived through decades of descendants. They are evidence of the passing of a tradition from one generation to the next and often sadly are the singular testimony to their often erudite makers. Such examples include those worked by Sarah Sherburne and her three daughters, Caroline, Harriet, and Catherine. Also included in this group are those worked by Hannah Cutter and her daughter, Hannah Cutter Rogers, and by Susannah Parker and her daughter, Elizabeth Toscan Parrott.

# Chronology of Sampler and Needlework Students and Their Work in Portsmouth, New Hampshire, 1741–1840

**Anna Green** (1728–1816)
*Sampler worked: 1741*
*Length: 20½ inches*
*Width: 8½ inches*
*Present owner: The Henry Francis du Pont Winterthur Museum*
Worked on unbleached linen in silk threads, three alphabets, and various decorative motifs including a central basket flanked by exotic plants and crowns are separated by horizontal crossbands. Within a pair of the crossbands is the verse:

> Behold alas Our days we Spend
> How Vain They be how Soon they end

and the legend ANNA GREEN HER SAMPLER 1741 PISCATAQUA.

Anna Green was the daughter of Anna Pierce (1700–1770) of Portsmouth, New Hampshire, and Joseph Green (1703–1765) of Boston, Massachusetts, who were married on December 28, 1727.[36] Anna married her cousin, Joshua Winslow (1726–1801), who was appointed a paymaster in the British forces in Nova Scotia on January 3, 1759.[37]

Their daughter, Anna Green Winslow (1759–1779), wrote *The Diary of Anna Green Winslow—A Boston School Girl of 1771*. The book was edited by Alice Morse Earle[38] and published in 1894, more than a century after young Anna's death, at the age of twenty, from consumption.

*Coat of arms worked by Prudence Penhallow about 1749. Courtesy of The Henry Francis du Pont Winterthur Museum.*

## Prudence Penhallow (1731–?)

*Coat of arms worked: circa 1749*
*Dimensions: Not known*
*Present owner: The Henry Francis du Pont Winterthur Museum*
Prudence Kneeland Penhallow was born in Boston in 1731 and probably learned to ply the needle in a Boston school. This coat of arms shows the arms of Penhallow impaling the arms of Kneeland and was most likely worked by Prudence prior to her marriage to Samuel Penhallow in 1749.

Her father-in-law, John Penhallow, of Portsmouth, married the widow of his former partner, John Watts. Penhallow was Clerk of the Superior Court in 1729 and died in 1735, leaving two sons, Samuel, who married Prudence Kneeland; and John Penhallow, who married Sarah Wentworth. Prudence and Samuel died without issue.[39]

## Sarah Sherburne (1748–1827)

*Sampler worked: circa 1760*
*Length: $19\frac{3}{4}$ inches*
*Width: $8\frac{1}{4}$ inches*
*Present owner: Portsmouth Historical Society*
Worked in silk on unbleached linen, the sampler includes a variety of horizontal crossbands that separate repetitions of the alphabet and enclose this verse:

> Sarah Sherburne is my name
> England is my nation
> Portsmouth is my dwelling place
> And Christ is my salvation.

Sarah was the daughter of Henry Sherburne (1709–1767) and Sarah Warner (1722), daughter of Daniel Warner. On March 18, 1765, our young needlework student, who was then seventeen years of age, married the Hon. Woodbury Langdon, brother of Gov. John Langdon. Both men served in the U.S. Senate. Woodbury gained fame as a judge in Portsmouth and the home that he built later became known as the Rockingham House, a portion of which survives today as the Rockingham Hotel Condominiums.[40]

Samplers worked by two of Sarah's daughters, Harriet and Caroline, also survive. (See their listings for 1790 and 1793.)

**Comfort Marshall** (1747–1788)
*Sampler worked: 1761*
*Length: 16½ inches*
*Width: 8¼ inches*
*Present owner: Jean Sawtelle*
On a band sampler with repetitions of the alphabet and numerals, Comfort included the following verse:

> Comfort Marshall Is My Name
> and England is my nation
> and Portsmouth is my Dwelling Place
> and Christ is my Salvation

At the base of the sampler is stitched: COMFORT MARSHALL/ BORN FEBRUARY 2 1747/ 14 BORN TUESDAY AT 10 AT NIGHT.

Comfort was probably the daughter of George Marshall, a sailmaker, and Thankful Weeks of Greenland, New Hampshire.[41] Comfort married Hopley Yeaton on November 15, 1766, in the old South Church in Portsmouth. They had seven children.

Yeaton was a captain and a veteran of the Continental navy. He was the first captain commissioned in the U.S. Revenue Marine Service. Comfort died in 1788. She was survived by five of her children.[42]

**Mary Stoodley** (1753–1784)
*Sampler worked: circa 1764*
*Length: 22 inches*
*Width: 16 inches*
*Present owner: unknown*
Seven repetitions of the alphabet are worked together with the Lord's Prayer enclosed with a strawberry design. An almost identical sampler, worked by Mary at age eleven, incorporated a floral motif in place of the strawberry design.

Mary was the daughter of James S. and Elizabeth Stoodley. On November 26, 1771, she married Nathaniel Folsom of Exeter, New Hampshire. She died at thirty-one years of age on May 27, 1784.[43] Her husband died in 1799.

Mary and Nathaniel had two children, Mary and Elizabeth (1774–1859). Mary married Thomas W. Rindge and Elizabeth married Capt. Joseph Noble.

**Mary Lonnergan** (1758–1830)
*Sampler worked: 1766*
*Length: 20¾ inches*
*Width: 7¾ inches*
*Present owner: Jean Sawtelle*
In a classic band sampler worked in silk on unbleached linen, Mary stitched several repetitions of the alphabet and numerals followed by the inscription:

> MARY LONNER
>
> GAN IS MY NAME
>
> NEW ENGLAND I
>
> S MY NATION P
>
> ORTSMOUTH IS
>
> MY DWELLING P
>
> LACE AND CHRI
>
> ST IS MY SALV
>
> ATION AUGUST
>
> 8 1766 AGE 8 YE
>
> ARS 2 3 4 5 6 7 8 9

Almost nothing is known about Mary Lonnergan other than Arthur H. Locke's 1907 reference in his *Portsmouth and New Castle Inscriptions* that her headstone could be found in the North Cemetery bearing the death date of December 18, 1830.

**Hannah Cutter** (1760–1840)
*Sampler worked: circa 1771*
*Length: 22½ inches*
*Width: 10¾ inches*
*Present owner: unknown*
Hannah's sampler includes trees, clover, and four repetitions of the alphabet.[44]

She was one of a dozen children of Dr. Ammi Ruhamah (1735–1820) and Hannah Treadwell Cutter (1734–1832). On October 1, 1780, Hannah married Daniel Rindge Rogers. The couple had one daughter, Hannah, who was born July 2, 1781.[45]

**Sarah Sevey** (1767–?)
*Sampler worked: 1773*
*Dimensions: unknown*
*Present owner: Society for the Preservation of New England Antiquities*
Sarah's sampler was worked in silk on unbleached linen with bands of alphabets and numerals and the verse:

> Sarah Sevey is/ My Name Engla/
> nd is My Nation. I/ S Portsmouth
> is my dwelling/ Place and Chri/st
> is my Salvati/on in the Year 1773.[46]

There can be little doubt that Portsmouth was the scene of Sarah's early education. On November 22, 1787, Sarah married Nathaniel Rand of Rye, New Hampshire.[47]

**Hetty Sheafe** (1760–1843)
*Sampler worked: circa 1773*
*Length: 20 inches*
*Width: 11 inches*
*Present owner: unknown*
Hetty worked her sampler with four alphabets interspersed with sixteen differing crossband designs.[48]
On May 5, 1785, Hetty (Mehitable) Sheafe, daughter of Jacob Sheafe, married the Hon. Ebenezer Smith of Durham, New Hampshire, an attorney. In 1798 he was appointed Judge of the Superior Court. He died September 24, 1831.[49]

**Sarah Hart** (1765–1842)
*Sampler worked: circa 1775*
*Length: 16½ inches*
*Width: 16 inches*
*Present owner: Portsmouth Historical Society*
Rendered in silk threads on a bleached linen ground, Sarah's sampler includes a vignette depicting Adam and Eve and the Tree of Life with a pastoral scene incorporating several animals. It is unique among Portsmouth samplers in that the motifs she chose are usually associated with ones worked considerably earlier in the century.

Sarah was the daughter of Richard Hart (1733–1820), the oldest son of Samuel and Bridget Cutt Hart. Richard married Mercy Collings of Kittery, Maine, on September 22, 1757. Mercy died July 17, 1790. Sarah never married.[50]

## Mary Stoodly (1773–?)

*Sampler worked: 1784*
*Length: 21½ inches*
*Width: 16⅜ inches*
*Present owner: Strawbery Banke Museum*

Worked in silk on unbleached linen, Mary Stoodly's sampler was composed of a series of repetitions of alphabets and numerals separated by a variety of sawtooth crossbands. In the lower portion of the sampler she signed her name and stitched her birth date, along with the date she completed the sampler, November 30, 1784.

Also included in the bottom section is the Lord's Prayer in cross-stitch with a final decorative arcade intermingled with strawberries and blossoms.

Mary Stoodly was the daughter of Guppy and Elizabeth Richardson Stoodly, who were married March 16, 1767. Their daughter was born on June 17, 1773.[51]

According to the U.S. Census for 1790, there were two Stoodly or Stoodley families in Portsmouth. Thomas Stoodly's household included only one female; Guppy Stoodly's included two. There are no announcements of Mary Stoodly's marriage or death to be found in Portsmouth newspapers between 1793 and 1800.

## Elizabeth Coues (1779–1838)

*Sampler worked: 1786*
*Length: 21½ inches*
*Width: 13½ inches*
*Present owner: Peter Coues*

Worked on unbleached linen, this sampler includes alphabets and numerals below which appears the familiar verse on virtue reminding the reader: "Virtue is the Chiefest Beauty of the Mind."

Elizabeth then stitched her name, ELIZABETH COUES WORK/ THIS IN OCTOBER 1786 IN TH/E 7 YEAR OF HER AGE. She also stitched the admonition: "Remember to keep such company as may improve you."

At the base of the sampler she centered a basket sprouting the stems of four flowers whose blossoms strongly resemble forms found in crewelworked embroidery. The basket is flanked by hillocks upon which are found plants and animals. The whole is enclosed within a tidy border of scrolls.

Elizabeth was the daughter of Peter and Elizabeth Jackson Coues and half sister of Charlotte Coues (sampler worked 1796), Caroline Coues (sampler worked circa 1797), and Maria Coues (sampler worked 1795). She also had ten other half brothers and sisters, the progeny of Peter Coues's three marriages.

On October 9, 1802, Elizabeth married Dr. Lyman Spalding, a medical graduate of Harvard University in the class of 1797. Together they had five children, among them Elizabeth Parkhurst Spalding, who operated a School for Young Ladies in Portsmouth in the 1830s. Lyman Spalding became a revered physician in Portsmouth. He died there in 1821.[52]

**Submit Boyd** (1774–1807)
*Coat of arms worked: 1787–1791*
*Dimensions: unknown*
*Present owner: anonymous*
Submit worked the Boyd coat of arms in silk and metal-wrapped threads. Acanthus leaves encompass the central arms-bearing shield.

This coat of arms was probably worked as a family tribute; it bears the arms of the Boyd family as well as those of her mother, Jane Brewster. It is believed that the piece was worked prior to Submit's marriage in 1791 to Samuel Sherburne, a Portsmouth attorney.

The epitaph Samuel later commissioned for his wife's tombstone at her death in 1807 at age twenty-eight concluded:

> Yet take these tears, immortality's relief,
> And till we share your joys forgive our grief
> These little rites, a tomb, a verse, receive;
> Tis all a husband, all a friend can give![53]

**Caroline Langdon** (1780–1865)
*Sampler worked: circa 1790*
*Length: 20 inches*

*Width: 12 inches*
*Present owner: Shirley-Eustis House Association*
Caroline's sampler in silk on linen showed four alphabets with various decorative elements including diamond shapes, a vine border, and the verse:

> The charms of Beauty soon will fade
> To Time must yield their power
> But Virtues Charms tho' Time invade
> Live to the latest hour.
> Thy choice Be Virtue then thy Guide her Charms
> Listen attentive to her guardian Voice
> Her bright example keep in constant view
> And all her precepts steadily pursue.
> Let Modesty (the females best defence)
> Sweetness of temper, Truth, Benevolence
> With all the virtues that true bliss impart
> Possess thy mind & ever rule thy heart.

Caroline was the daughter of the Hon. Woodbury Langdon and Sarah Sherburne Langdon, who worked a sampler in 1760 that is now in the Portsmouth Historical Society collections.

On September 24, 1810, Caroline married William Eustis of Boston, Massachusetts. He was Secretary of War under both President Jefferson and President Madison, and became governor of Massachusetts in 1824.[54]

The mansion in which they lived still stands in Roxbury, Massachusetts, and is a historic property open to the public. The couple had no children. When Caroline died, in 1865, the contents of her house were sold at public auction.

**Susannah Parker** (1780–1852)
*Sampler worked: 1790*
*Length: 14 inches*
*Width: 9 inches*
*Present owner: Mrs. Merrill Spalding*
Susannah worked several repetitions of the alphabet in eyelet and cross-stitch, enclosing them within a vine border and marked "Portsmouth" as her home.

She married Capt. Enoch G. Parrott in 1809 and the couple had three children. Enoch Parrott died in 1828, twenty-four years before Susannah, who died April 21, 1852.[55] Their daughter Elizabeth Toscan Parrott worked a sampler in 1829.

### Ann Huske Sheafe (1781–1875)

*Coat of arms worked: 1791*
*Length: 18 inches*
*Width: 16 inches*
*Present owner: Portsmouth Athenaeum*

Ann's coat of arms is composed of painted silk with gold foil. Three sheaves of wheat, depicted in foil, are enclosed within a painted shield.

She was the daughter of Jacob Sheafe, Jr., of Portsmouth, and she married Charles Cushing, a prosperous Portsmouth merchant. Ann and Charles Cushing occupied the Gov. Benning Wentworth mansion at Little Harbor in Portsmouth from 1817 until Ann's death in 1875. The couple had five children.[56]

### Lydia Peirce (1780–1844)

*Sampler worked: 1792*
*Length: 22 inches*
*Width: 11½ inches*
*Present owner: The Warner House Association*

Worked on unbleached linen, the lower portion of Lydia Peirce's sampler includes strawberries set against a solid background of green silk cross-stitch. A variety of crossband designs separate the lines of the repetitions of the alphabet while the legend LYDIA PEIRCE HER SAMPLER AGED 12 YEARS/ PORTSMOUTH SEPTEMBER 11 1792 appears at the bottom of the sampler.

The receipt illustrated here shows that Lydia went on to teach others. The document, in the archives of the Thayer Cumings Historical Reference Library at Strawbery Banke, is a bill to Mary Chase for the "schooling" of her granddaughters Mary Tappan and Harriet Crosby in the summer of 1809.[57]

Miss Lydia Peirce died unmarried at the age of sixty-four in 1844, "a humble and devoted Christian."[58]

**Harriet Langdon** (1785–1815)
*Sampler worked: 1793*
*Length: 21 inches*
*Width: 11¾ inches*
*Present owner: Portsmouth Historical Society*
Among the decorative elements that Harriet Langdon worked in silk on unbleached linen in the lower portion of her sampler are a basket of delicately rendered flowers and a bee and a butterfly. This arrangement is flanked by a mounded strawberry plant on the left and a squirrel on the right.

The verse Harriot chose appears in its earliest use on a Portsmouth sampler but proved to be popular with needleworkers almost universally. It reads:

> How blest the maid who circling years improve
> Her God the object of her warmest love.
> Whose useful hours successive as they glide
> The book, the needle and the Pen divide.

She was eight years old at the time she worked her sampler. Her sister Caroline worked a sampler three years earlier and their mother, Sarah Sherburne, worked hers in 1760. Harriot did not marry and died at the age of thirty in 1815.[59]

**Hannah Cutter Rogers** (1781–1847)
*Sampler worked: 1793*
*Length: 16½ inches*
*Width: 12½ inches*
*Present owner: unknown*
Hannah's sampler is recorded as being composed of three repetitions of the alphabet within a border of trefoil and roses at the sides, scrolls at the top, and a wide floral design at the base.[61]

She was born on July 2, 1781, the daughter of Hannah Cutter and Daniel Rindge Rogers, who had married on October 1, 1780. Hannah's mother had worked a sampler some twenty-two years earlier in 1771. Hannah married Lemuel Draper, a Portsmouth merchant, and died in Portsmouth in March 1847.[62]

**Sally White** (1783–1798)
*Sampler worked: 1795*
*Length: 14 inches*
*Width: 12¼ inches*
*Present owner: unknown*
Sally White's sampler has four repetitions of the alphabet enclosed by a vine border and a pair of flower-filled baskets separated by an elaborate floral design.

  She was the daughter of Nathaniel White, of Portsmouth. Sally worked the sampler at the age of eleven. Four years later, at fifteen, she died in Newburyport, Massachusetts.[63]

**Maria Coues** (1788–1797)
*Sampler worked: 1795*
*Length: 17 inches*
*Width: 12¼ inches*
*Present owner: Mrs. John Foster*
Working in silk on unbleached linen, Maria stitched a sampler within an arcaded border that includes repetitions of the alphabet and numerals.

  Below this she stitched four lines of verse and her name, along with a notation of her age (seven) and the year 1795. Maria decorated the base of the sampler with a pair of flowering trees and branches.

  She was the daughter of Peter Coues and Rebecca Elliott Coues.

**Charlotte Coues** (1787–1809)
*Sampler worked: 1796*
*Length: 20½ inches*
*Width: 18¼ inches*
*Present owner: Peter Coues*
Working on unbleached linen, Charlotte put together a sampler composed of the required alphabets and numerals along with four lines of verse extolling virtue. Also included are her name, "CHARLOTTE COUES 1796 aged 8," and a pleasing assortment of flora, birds, and insects that decorate the base, the whole enclosed in a lively arcaded border with strawberries.

  Charlotte was the daughter of Peter and Rebecca Elliott Coues and sister of Caroline (sampler worked 1797) and Maria (sampler worked 1795). Because Peter was married three times, Charlotte was part of a large extended family that included her half sister Elizabeth (sampler worked 1786).

Charlotte died at the age of twenty-two in February 1809. Fortunately, a rare survival among the artifacts associated with the women whose samplers survive has been passed down in this instance. A silhouette of Charlotte gives us a glimpse of the person who stitched this sampler.

### Caroline Coues (1791–1813)

*Sampler worked: circa 1797*
*Length: 12 inches*
*Width: 7 inches*
*Present owner: Peter Coues*

Following a conventional format, Caroline stitched a simple and plain sampler composed of repetitions of the alphabet and numerals within a meandering border. Worked on green linsey-woolsey, she simply signed her name within the lowermost portion of the sampler.

Caroline was one of thirteen children born to Peter Coues (1736–1818) of Portsmouth. She was the daughter of his third wife, Rebecca Elliott (1762–1799), half sister of Elizabeth Coues (sampler worked 1786), and aunt to Elizabeth's daughter Adelaide (sampler worked circa 1814).[64]

### Elizabeth Tredick (1789–1815)

*Sampler worked: 1799*
*Length: 11 inches*
*Width: 16 inches*
*Present owner: anonymous*

Elizabeth worked her sampler in about 1799 in silk on linen. It includes repetitions of the alphabet and numerals in the upper portion and a depiction of Adam and Eve in the lower portion. The couple flank a tree with an entwined serpent. Surrounding them all are renderings of birds, angels, and animals. The whole is enclosed within a meandering arcaded border.

She also included the verse, "Elizabeth Tredick is my name and with my needle I worked the same age 10." The daughter of Henry and Margaret Tredick, she married George Kennard. Elizabeth died at the age of twenty-six on October 10, 1815.[65]

**Mary Langdon** (1788–?)
*Sampler worked: 1800*
*Length: 22 inches*
*Width: 17 inches*
*Present owner: Old York Historical Society, York, Maine*
Mary Langdon's sampler in silk on unbleached linen shares similarities with those worked by Henrietta Tuttell (1803), Abigail Bowles (1804), Martha Gaines (1804), Mary Gerrish (1811), Sarah Catherine Moffatt Odiorne (1806), and Mary Elizabeth Coffin (1814).

Enclosed within a two-color, banded border Mary worked alphabets and numerals in the upper portion of the sampler. A multicolored crossband of a flame-stitch-like pattern forms the separation between upper and lower sections of the needlework. Below this, Mary centered a cartouche in black threads, forming a memorial to George Washington. This is flanked by smaller cartouches that contain the alphabet and the initials ACI (left) and the inscription MARY/ LANGDON AG/ED 12 1800/ FEAR GOD (right). Below these she stitched a tasseled swag in black.

Under the swag Mary stitched in black threads a verse that is no longer legible. The verse is framed by a pair of trees whose boughs spread out over the verse, stretching up toward the swag. An undulating landscape of green hillocks fills in the base.

In Rev. Alden's catalog printed in 1808 he included two Mary Langdons, one of whom lived in Newington while the other lived in Portsmouth. In fact, Mary Langdon was probably a pupil in one of the first years of the Alden Academy. It was the Mary Langdon who lived on Russell Street in Portsmouth with her mother, Mary, who made this sampler.[66] She was the daughter of John (1749–1789) and Mary Evans Langdon. According to the 1790 census, John and Mary had four daughters. All but Mary married; the City Directory for 1821 indicates that she lived with her widowed mother on Russell Street. By the time of the printing of the 1827 directory, Mary was living alone at the same address.

*Sampler worked by Sarah Sherburne before 1765; she gives the date of her birth on the sampler–March 27, 1748. Collections of the Portsmouth Historical Society.*

*Sampler worked by Sarah Hart, circa 1775. Collections of Portsmouth Historical Society. Dan Gair photograph.*

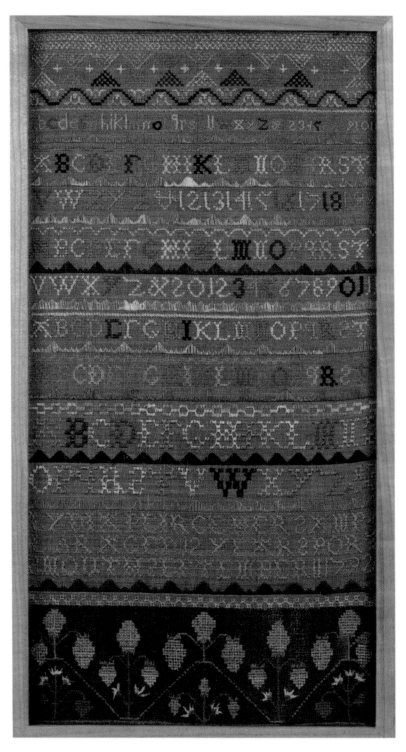

*Sampler worked by Lydia Peirce in 1792. Collections of the Warner House Association. Dan Gair photograph.*

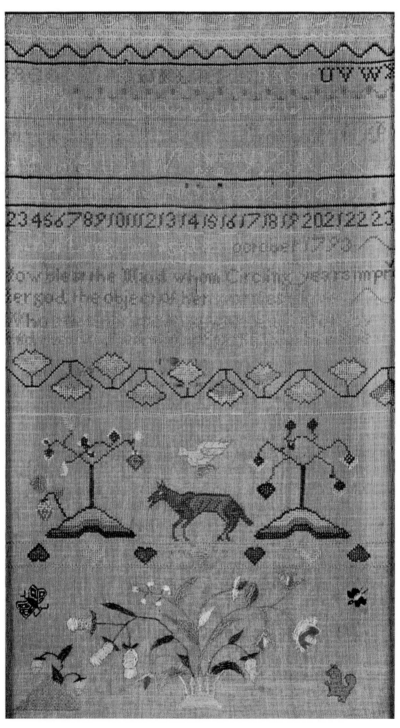

*Sampler worked in 1793 by Harriet Langdon. Collections of the Portsmouth Historical Society. Dan Gair photograph.*

*Sampler worked by Henrietta Tuttell in 1803. Collections of Rita F. Conant. Dan Gair photograph.*

*Sampler worked by Lucretia Tarlton in 1807. Collection of Jean Sawtelle.*

*Sampler worked by Eliza Jane Salter in 1808. Collection of Jean Sawtelle.*

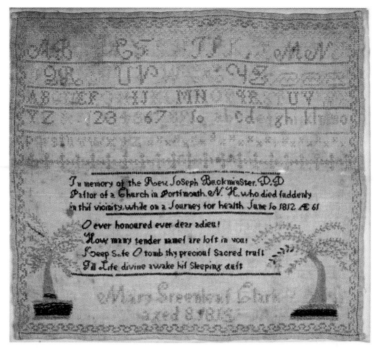

*Sampler worked by Mary Greenleaf Clark in 1815. Collection of Jean Sawtelle.*

*Sampler worked by Mary Catherine Evans in 1818. Collection of Jean Sawtelle.*

*Sampler worked in 1817 by Elizabeth Lake. Collections of the Portsmouth Historical Society. Dan Gair photograph.*

*Sampler worked by Elizabeth Fernald in 1818. Collection of Jean Sawtelle.*

*Sampler worked in 1840 by Sarah Emily Currier. Collections of the Portsmouth Historical Society. Dan Gair photograph.*

*Sampler worked by Harriet Ann Dockum in 1825. Collection of Jean Sawtelle.*

*Sampler worked by Ann Elizabeth Ham in 1826. Collection of Jean Sawtelle.*

*Sampler worked by Mary Ann Marden in 1828. Collection of Jean Sawtelle.*

*Sampler worked by Mary A. Shapleigh in 1831. Collection of Jean Sawtelle.*

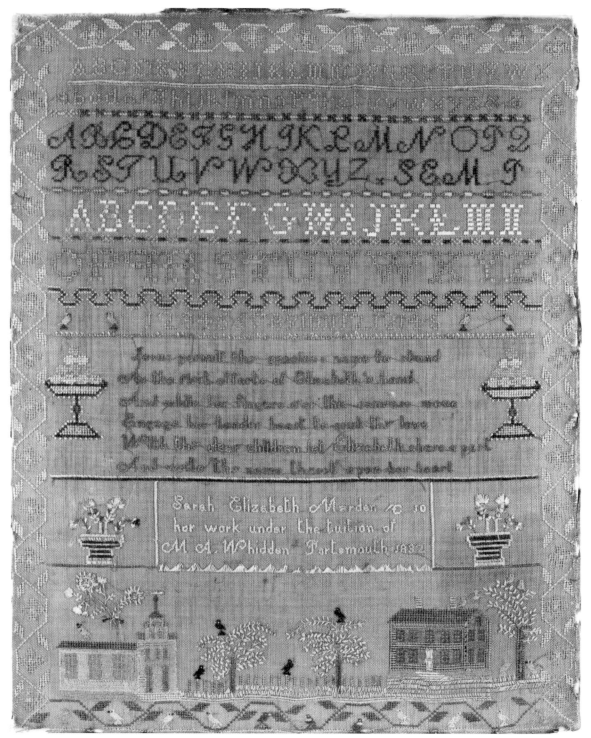

*Sampler worked by Sarah Elizabeth Marden in 1832. Collection of Jean Sawtelle.*

*Sampler worked in 1834 by Elizabeth Fabyan Willey. Collections of the Portsmouth Historical Society. Dan Gair photograph.*

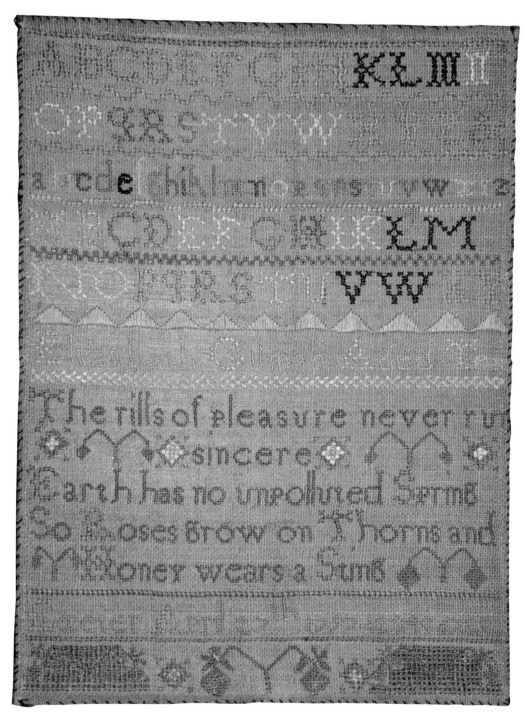

*Sampler worked in 1797 by Elizabeth Gilman. Collections of the Portsmouth Historical Society. Photograph by Alan Haesche.*

*Sampler by Deborah Laighton, dated October 15, 1818/19, worked at Mary Ann Smith's School. Collections of the Portsmouth Historical Society; gift of Ron Bourgeault and Elizabeth Sturges in memory of Merrilee Possner. Photograph courtesy of Northeast Auctions.*

*Sampler worked in 1821 by Mary Harvey. Collections of the Portsmouth Historical Society. Photograph by Alan Haesche.*

*Two samplers worked by Ann Pierce Drown—one dated June 1829 and the other*
*September 10 without a year. Collections of the Portsmouth Historical Society.*
*Photograph by Alan Haesche.*

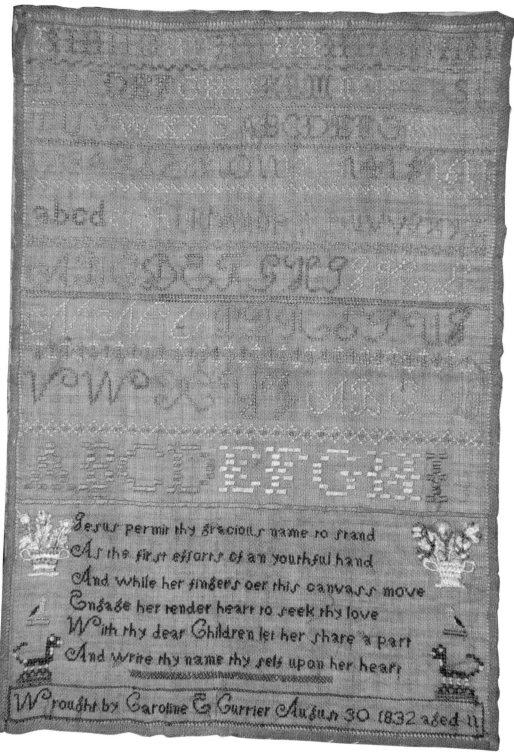

*Sampler worked in 1832 by Caroline Currier. Collections of the Portsmouth Historical Society. Photograph by Alan Haesche.*

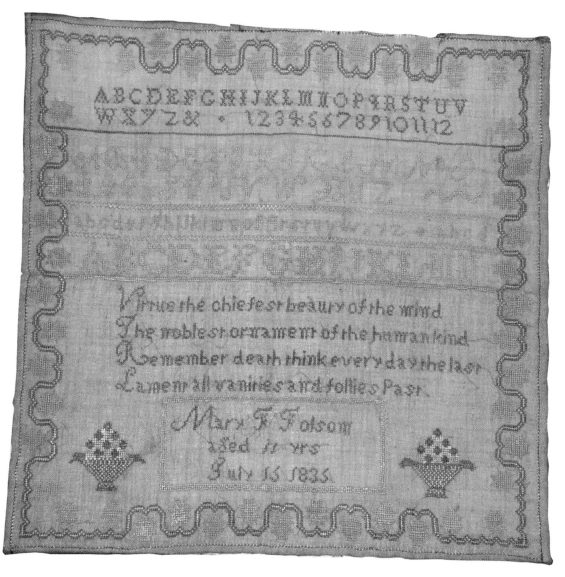

*Sampler worked in 1835 by Mary Frances Folsom. Collections of the Portsmouth Historical Society. Photograph by Alan Haesche.*

*Sampler worked in 1801 by Sally Breed, Lynn, Massachusetts. She married William Ilsley and lived in Portsmouth from the early 1820s. Collections of the Portsmouth Historical Society. Photograph by Alan Haesche.*

*Sampler worked by Susan Stodder. Gift of Mrs. William B. Trask [Susan Ellen Walker], who was born in Portsmouth. Collections of the Portsmouth Historical Society. Photograph by Alan Haesche.*

**Martha Nutter** (1789–1861)
*Sampler worked: 1800*
*Length: 16 inches*
*Width: 12¾ inches*
*Present owner: Strawbery Banke Museum*
Martha Nutter worked her sampler in silk threads on unbleached linen. She stitched several bands of repetitions of the alphabet and the notation MARTHA NUTTER HER SAMPLER AGED 10 1800. She also include a verse that is now only partially legible.

She married Thomas Darling Bailey and had five children, one of whom, Sara Aba, was the mother of the noted nineteenth-century author Thomas Bailey Aldrich.[67]


**Jane Clark Haslett** (1788–?)
*Sampler worked: 1801*
*Length: 16⅓ inches*
*Width: 8⅓ inches*
*Present owner: Strawbery Banke Museum*
Silk threads on unbleached linen were used to cross-stitch several repetitions of the alphabet and numerals, along with the legend JANE CLARK HASLETT HER SAMPLER AGED 13 and the verse,

> Jane Haslett is my name
> New England is my nation
> Portsmouth is my dwelling place.

The April 1766 issue of the *New Hampshire Gazette* announced the arrival in Portsmouth from Boston of the Haslett brothers, James and nineteen-year-old Matthew, who established their "factory" at the sign of the Buck and Glove adjacent to Canoe Bridge.[68] They were leather dressers whose place of business near Canoe Bridge stood at the edge of Puddle Dock in the present-day Strawbery Banke Museum site. In 1773 Matthew dissolved the partnership with his brother and the following year married Ann Frost on December 3. Their daughter, Jane Clark Haslett, was born June 8, 1788. Matthew died at forty-five years of age in 1792.[69]

**Catherine Whipple Langdon** (1788–1809)
*Sampler worked: 1801*
*Dimensions: unknown*
*Present owner: unknown*

Catherine was the daughter of Woodbury Langdon and Sarah Sherburne Langdon. On September 10, 1808, she married Edmund Roberts in Portsmouth. She was then twenty years old.

Five years earlier Catherine penned a journal. Her journal is rich in the details of daily life in Portsmouth in the early nineteenth century: of familial relationships and friendships, and of both the joy and sorrow she experienced. Because she felt the strong impulse to record her daily routine, we are today blessed with a rare personal glimpse into a life lived more than 150 years ago.

Edmund Roberts had been orphaned at the age of sixteen and was raised by a successful merchant uncle in Buenos Aires. After his uncle's death, Roberts returned to Portsmouth, where he met and married Catherine and carried on his business, which eventually failed due to the rigors of trade with Europe.

Because members of Catherine's family were politically well placed (a close relative, Levy Woodbury, was Secretary of the Navy under President Jackson), her husband was successful in convincing Washington insiders of the merits of pursuing trade agreements with Far Eastern countries. He succeeded in opening up trade for American merchants through treaties signed with Muscat and Siam and was en route to Japan when he died of an unrecorded illness in Macao.

Catherine and Edmund had eleven children.[60]


**Ann Lewis Parry** (1787–1825)
*Silk memorial picture worked: 1802*
*Length: $12\frac{3}{4}$ inches*
*Width: 10 inches*
*Present owner: anonymous*

Ann Parry made this finely worked memorial to her father, Capt. Martin Parry, entirely in silk, drawing the face and arms in ink. He had fallen victim to yellow fever in the summer of 1802 at the age of forty-four. Martin Parry was a merchant of considerable standing and also acted as the agent for the Salem, Massachusetts, shipowner William Gray, Esq., whose vessels were loading at Portsmouth piers for India, Russia, and numerous other destinations.[70] The inscription on the memorial tomb reads:

To/The Memory/ of/
A Loved Regreted/ Father/ Mr. Martin
Parry/ Obit July 29th 1802/ AE 44/
This Is Inscribed/ By His/
Affectionate Dau TR/A. Parry.

Ann Lewis Parry was born to Capt. Martin Parry and Ann Simes Parry, the daughter of Joseph Simes. For a time Martin Parry worked as silversmith, watchmaker, and jeweler, as well as at an assortment of other mercantile interests. The Portsmouth silversmith William Simes was apprenticed to him. In December 1808 Ann married William Jones, Esq., who, like his father-in-law, was a successful Portsmouth merchant, with a dry goods establishment on Market Street that he operated for nearly 20 years.

Their children were William Parry Jones, born in 1811, and Ann Simes Jones, born in 1813. Both lived long lives, dying in 1872 and 1891, respectively. In 1821 Ann Simes Jones completed a sampler that is also recorded here. Their mother, Ann Parry Jones, died in 1825 at the age of thirty-seven and their father remarried in the same year. Their stepmother was Ann G. Lunt, the eldest daughter of Capt. Thomas Lunt.[71]

## Henrietta Tuttell (1796–1862)
*Sampler worked: 1803*
*Length: 23 inches*
*Width: 18¾ inches*
*Present owner: Rita F. Conant*
Worked in silk on linen, Henrietta's sampler shares design motifs found in the Sara Catherine Moffatt Odiorne sampler stitched at Miss Ward's School in 1806.

Within a border of solid cross-stitch, Henrietta worked three repetitions of the alphabet followed by a crossband of a flame-stitch-like pattern in a variety of colors. This motif creates a dividing line for the verse and other decorative elements that occupy the lower half of the sampler.

A memorial urn appears at the upper center of the lower portion, flanked by ovoid tablets containing the alphabet and the inscription HENRIETTA TUTTELL AGED 8 1803 123456789 AE 10. Under the urn appears the memorial verse to her brother Hugh Hunter Tuttell, who died in 1798 at seven months:

*Sampler worked by Sally Blunt in 1804. Collection of Betty Ring.*
*Allen Mewbourn photograph.*

Sweet Seraph Boy! a Short adieu!
'Tis but a moment and I come
Where my lov'd Brother makes his home,
Above you worlds of azure blue!
Remember thy Creator in the days of
thy youth childhood and youth are vanity.

The base of the sampler is decorated with a landscape composed of a simply wrought tree and shrubbery along with trailing sprays of rosebuds.

Henrietta was the daughter of Hugh Hunter and Priscilla Hazard Tuttell. In 1823 she married William L. Martine, a ship's captain. The couple had three sons. Henrietta died in 1862 in Dorchester, Massachusetts, and was buried in Harmony Grove Cemetery on South Street in Portsmouth.[72]

## Martha Gaines (1794–?)

*Sampler worked: 1804*
*Length: 26 inches*
*Width: 16¼ inches*
*Present owner: Newington Historical Society*

Working with silk on linen, Martha stitched a sampler enclosed by an arcaded border entwined with vines and with a bluebird perched at the very top. Below are a series of alphabets and numerals. At the midpoint a crossband in a pattern resembling the flame stitch separates the alphabet and numerals above from the verse and cartouche, with her name and completion date below. These same elements appear in the samplers made by Henrietta Tuttell (1803) and Mary Langdon (1800).

She chose to stitch a verse entitled "On Friendship," which is flanked by a pair of small flower baskets above the cartouche itself flanked by a pair of bluebirds. Across the bottom of the sampler and the green landscape sprout strawberry plants.

Martha was the daughter of George and Sarah Pickering Gaines of Newington, New Hampshire. Her grandfather was John Gaines, the well-known joiner who produced stylish furniture for Portsmouth patrons.[73]

**Sally Blunt** (1795–1880)
*Sampler worked: 1804*
*Length: 31½ inches*
*Width: 17½ inches*
*Present owner: Betty Ring*
Sally's sampler, worked in silk on green linsey-woolsey, includes the repetition of the alphabet and numerals along with several other distinctive features and this verse:

> How blest the maid whom circling years improve
> Her God the object of her warmest love
> Whose active years successive as they glide
> The Book the Needle and the Pen divide.

Sally (Sarah) was the daughter of Capt. Robert W. Blunt and Elizabeth Sherburne, who were married by the Rev. Samuel Haven in March 1792.[74] Their home on Washington Street in Portsmouth is now known as the Leonard Cotton House.

In 1824 Sally married William Chase, then a merchant in Portsmouth, who lived only a few doors away in a house that is now part of the Strawbery Banke Museum, the Stephen Chase House. William and Sally were married in South Church by the Rev. Dr. Parker.[75]

As a child, Sally attended the Rev. Timothy Alden's academy, as did her classmate Mary Ann Hooker, and each completed samplers, a year apart, while they were pupils there. The nearly identical samplers employed the unusual device of a scallop shell within which were their names and ages. Each of the scallop shells is also flanked by baskets holding mounded fruit.

Without a doubt the designs for the girls' work was set out by the same teacher. In 1807, it is recorded that Sally completed a needlework picture at the school entitled "Emblem of America," probably modeled after an illustration published in London in 1800.[76]

After Sally's death in 1880 at the age of eighty-five, her nephew, George Chase, son of her brother-in-law Theodore Chase, purchased her house on Court and Washington Streets and donated the property as the Chase Home for Children. Over the years, many of the objects from the house were dispersed, including Sally's sampler.

**Abigail (Nabby) Bowles** (1793–1821)
*Sampler worked: 1804*
*Length: 20 inches*
*Width: 15½ inches*
*Present owner: Joan Hammond*
Working in silk on linen, Nabby Bowles made a sampler that shares design motifs found in the one worked by Henrietta Tuttell in 1803, and in those stitched by Mary Langdon in 1800 and Martha Gaines in 1804, Sarah Catherine Moffatt Odiorne in 1806, Mary Gerrish in 1811, and Mary Elizabeth Coffin in 1814.

Nabby stitched three repetitions of the alphabet. The upper portion of her sampler contains a pair of small baskets filled with flowers, a pair of cherubs, and a pair of peacocks. In the lower portion she stitched a willow tree in green and flanked it with a pair of ovoid tablets on which she filled the inscriptions NABBY BOWLES AGED 11 1804 REMEMBER THY CREATOR, and THE LORD IS GOOD UNTO ALL AND HIS TENDER MERCIES ARE OVER ALL HIS WORKS. The base of the sampler is decorated with a landscape composed of trees and shrubbery.

In 1806, 1807, and 1808 Nabby was a student at Rev. Timothy Alden's academy where it was noted that in 1807 she worked on a mourning scene.[77]

Nabby was the daughter of Capt. John Bowles (a charter member of The Portsmouth Marine Society) and Lydia Bowles, who lived on North Street, now named Maplewood Avenue.

**Elizabeth Langdon** (1795–1875)
*Sampler worked: 1805*
*Length: 17 inches*
*Width: 17½ inches*
*Present owner: Newington Historical Society*
Stitching with silk on linen, Elizabeth Langdon worked repetitions of the alphabet and numerals, filling the upper portion of her sampler. Below them, she stitched a pair of baskets with mounded fruit that flank the verse:

> This work in hand
> My friends may have
> When I am dead
> And in my Grave.

*Sampler worked by Mary Ann Hooker in 1805. Private collection. Photograph courtesy Sheila and Edwin Rideout.*

She also stitched her signature, WROUGHT BY ELIZABETH LANG-DON PORTSMOUTH N.H.

Elizabeth was the daughter of Rev. Joseph and Patience Pickering Langdon of Newington, New Hampshire. She married Samuel Whidden III in March 1827. Both died in 1875, he in January and she in December. They had five children.[78]

**Mary Ann Hooker** (1794–1868)
*Sampler worked: 1805*
*Length: 31¾ inches*
*Width: 16¾ inches*
*Present owner: anonymous*
Worked in silk on green linsey-woolsey, Mary Ann's sampler is composed of four alphabets and one row of numerals followed by the verse:

> How blest the Maid whom circling years improve
> Her God the object of her warmest love
> Whose active years successive as they glide
> The Book the Needle and the Pen divide.

Just as Sally Blunt did, Mary Ann included the distinctive scallop shell and baskets laden with fruit. She chose, however, not to fill out the remaining lower section of the sampler with trees, birds, and a basket but instead stitched in the adage "Beauty is a fading flower" in one corner and "Virtue is a blooming flower" to fill the lower corners. Records of Reverend Alden's academy indicate that Mary Ann was in attendance there in at least 1803, 1806, and 1807 and that she was taught "embroidery" there. In 1807 she completed a silk picture at Alden's academy entitled "These Are My Jewels."[79]

The daughter of Capt. Michael Hooker, Mary Ann married a rather successful Portsmouth merchant named Ichabod Rollins on November 2, 1818, and they took up residence in a house on Pleasant Street.[74] Portraits of both Mary Ann and her husband are now in the collection of the Portsmouth Historical Society at the John Paul Jones House.

**Sarah Wentworth Austin** (1794–1865)
*Sampler worked: 1805*
*Dimensions: unknown*
*Present owner: unknown*
Sarah was the daughter of Mary Penhallow and Daniel Austin, Esq., who had been married on July 22, 1787. Sarah never married but her one brother, Daniel (1793–1877), married Hannah Joy in 1833.[81]

Sarah W. Austin, with her brother, opened a school for young ladies and gentlemen where needlework was taught to the ladies.

**Sarah Catherine Moffatt Odiorne** (1794–1870)
*Sampler worked: circa 1806*
*Dimensions: unknown*
*Present owner: unknown*
Illustrated by Bolton and Coe in their book *American Samplers*, this sampler appears to have been worked in silk on unbleached linen. Sarah more or less divided her sampler in half and proceeded to work the design elements almost as though they were a pair of samplers joined within a common border.[82]

The upper half of the sampler has the Ten Commandments at its center, flanked by vine-encircled verses, each with a flower spray at the bottom and a bird perched in the branches above. Repetitions of the alphabet fill the remaining space in the upper half.

A strong line of decorative stitches separates this from the lower portion, which has a centered urn on a pedestal bearing the initials SCM. At its base is the legend IN MEMORY OF MRS. SARAH CATHERINE MOFFATT OBIT. DECEMBER [?] 1802 AE. This in turn is flanked by floral wreaths enclosing cartouches with legends including SARAH CATHERINE MOFFATT ODIORNE/ AGED 12 1806 WORKED AT/ MISS WARDS SCHOOL/ PORTSMOUTH NEW HAMP/SHIRE FEAR GOD HONOR/ YOUR PARENTS. She also worked verses in the second cartouche. According to *The Odiorne Family Genealogy*, Sarah was the daughter of William and was born in Kittery, Maine, in 1794. She married Andrew Leighton, also of Kittery, in December 1814.[83]

On her mother's side, she was descended from John Mason, the original grantee of the Province of New Hampshire. Her father's ancestors built the Manor House at Odiorne's Point in Rye, New Hampshire.

**Mary Macpheadris Warner Conner** (1797–1886)
*Sampler worked: 1806*
*Dimensions: unknown*
*Present owner: unknown*
This sampler was worked in silk on green linsey-woolsey and was finished in February 1806. According to a twentieth-century account of Mary's childhood by a descendant who owned the sampler, Mary attended a private school in The Academy, and was "a dainty child and sometimes, as she hesitated to cross muddy Market Street in her little slippers, a young lawyer, Daniel Webster by name, would pick her up and carry her across on his strong shoulders."

The sampler she worked was described by her granddaughter as having the alphabet and the verse:

> Be good, dear child, and ease they parents' care
> Choose to be wise, rather than fair.
> Abstain from those who would thy youth betray
> and from the path of virtue never stray

All was enclosed within a "border of pink flowers, in Kensington stitch." Mary was the daughter of Abigail Warner and Benjamin Connor and lived in the Macpheadris Warner House on Daniel Street in Portsmouth.[84]

**Lucretia Tarlton** (1793–1868)
*Sampler worked: 1807*
*Length: $23\frac{1}{4}$ inches*
*Width: 16 inches*
*Present owner: Jean Sawtelle*
On green linsey-woolsey Lucretia worked bands of the alphabet and numerals in silk decorative stitches. At the central portion of the sampler is a geometric form flanked by left-facing birds, figure eights of chain stitch, and conical-shaped trees in green cross-stitch followed by the legend:

> When this you se remember me and bar
> me in mind let all the world Sa what
> thay will Speeck of me as you find
> Lucretia Tarltons sampler Marked by

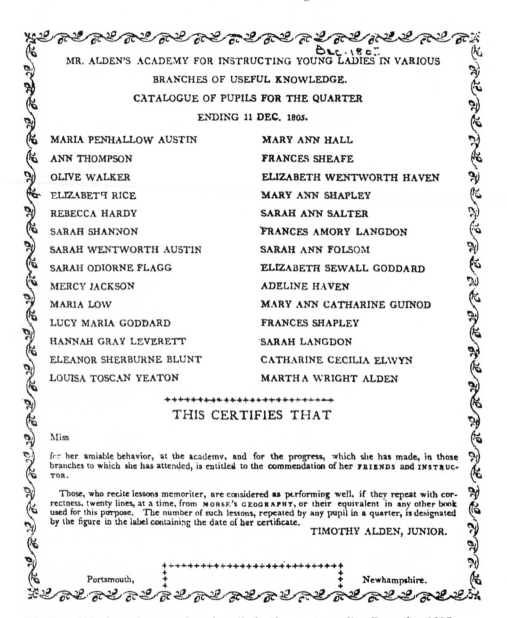

Dec. 1805

MR. ALDEN'S ACADEMY FOR INSTRUCTING YOUNG LADIES IN VARIOUS
BRANCHES OF USEFUL KNOWLEDGE.

CATALOGUE OF PUPILS FOR THE QUARTER

ENDING 11 DEC. 1805.

| | |
|---|---|
| MARIA PENHALLOW AUSTIN | MARY ANN HALL |
| ANN THOMPSON | FRANCES SHEAFE |
| OLIVE WALKER | ELIZABETH WENTWORTH HAVEN |
| ELIZABETH RICE | MARY ANN SHAPLEY |
| REBECCA HARDY | SARAH ANN SALTER |
| SARAH SHANNON | FRANCES AMORY LANGDON |
| SARAH WENTWORTH AUSTIN | SARAH ANN FOLSOM |
| SARAH ODIORNE FLAGG | ELIZABETH SEWALL GODDARD |
| MERCY JACKSON | ADELINE HAVEN |
| MARIA LOW | MARY ANN CATHARINE GUINOD |
| LUCY MARIA GODDARD | FRANCES SHAPLEY |
| HANNAH GRAY LEVERETT | SARAH LANGDON |
| ELEANOR SHERBURNE BLUNT | CATHARINE CECILIA ELWYN |
| LOUISA TOSCAN YEATON | MARTHA WRIGHT ALDEN |

++++++++++++++++++++++++++

THIS CERTIFIES THAT

Miss

for her amiable behavior, at the academy, and for the progress, which she has made, in those
branches to which she has attended, is entitled to the commendation of her FRIENDS and INSTRUC-
TOR.

Those, who recite lessons memoriter, are considered as performing well, if they repeat with correctness, twenty lines, at a time, from MORSE'S GEOGRAPHY, or their equivalent in any other book
used for this purpose. The number of such lessons, repeated by any pupil in a quarter, is designated
by the figure in the label containing the date of her certificate.

TIMOTHY ALDEN, JUNIOR.

++++++++++++++++++++++++++

Portsmouth,                                                    Newhampshire.

*The Rev. Alden's academy catalog of pupils for the quarter ending December 1805.*

Hir July in the year of our lord 1807 aged 14
yers old born may the 16.

Lucretia's father was William Tarlton, who was born in New
Castle in 1763. He worked as skipper of a small vessel. In 1786 he
married Lucretia Amazeen. Lucretia was the third of their six children. In 1815 she married Reuben Sanborn, of Epsom, New Hampshire, who owned a small farm. After her husband's death in 1853,
she moved to Haverhill, Massachusetts, where she lived until her
death in 1868 at age 74.[85]

## *The Reverend Timothy Alden Academy*

Timothy Alden operated his Academy in Portsmouth for some seven
years, from early in 1801 to 1808. For a number of years he issued a
"catalogue" of his students and their accomplishments in a myriad of
subjects. For at least some of those years the misses who attended and
received instruction in needlework were identified by a letter code
that included "e" for embroidery, "m" for working in muslin, and "p"
for those who "attend to painting." He further identified the students
who worked silk pictures in the year 1807 with the titles of their
work, all of which seemed to have been drawn from printed sources
widely available in the period. We have here identified the students
according to Alden's 1806 and 1807 catalogs, adding the type of
needlework in which they received instruction. Our list is alphabetical
and we have combined the names from the two years.

Ann Hall Adams, embroidery, painting
Ann Bagnell, painting
Elizabeth A. Bagnell, painting
Abigail Ballard, painting
Abigail Bowles, embroidery (Mourning Scene)
Eleanor S. Blunt, embroidery (These Are My Jewels), painting
Elizabeth Blunt, working muslin
Mary Ann Blunt, embroidery, painting (Flora)
Elizabeth H. Clarke, painting
Mary Ann Chandler, embroidery
Ann Drisco, embroidery (Melpomene)
Isabella S. Fernald, embroidery, working muslin

Lydia Gerrish, embroidery (Mourning Scene)
Mary Mills Glidden, painting
Lucy Maria Goddard, painting
Martha Goodhue, embroidery
Mary Ann Hall, embroidery, painting
Charlotte Ann Haven, embroidery (Melpomene)
Caroline Haven, embroidery, painting
Elizabeth W. Haven, embroidery (Landscape)
Mehetabel Hilton, embroidery
Mary Ann Hooker, embroidery, painting (These Are My Jewels)
Mercy Jackson, embroidery, painting
Elizabeth Hill Jones, embroidery, painting
Ann Kennard, painting
Mary Langdon, working muslin
Maria Low, embroidery
Mary Ann Low, embroidery (Mourning Scene)
Jane B. Mackay, working muslin
Alice S. Manning, embroidery
Sarah Ann Manning, embroidery (Mourning Scene)
Frances A. C. March, working muslin, painting
Margaret F. Mead, embroidery, painting (Landscape)
Mary Ann Means, painting
Catharine H. Melcher, embroidery
Jane Norie, embroidery
Sarah W. Penhallow, embroidery
Ann Lewis Parry, working muslin
Sarah A. E. Rice, embroidery (Youth Instructed in Geography)
Ann Weeks Rollins, embroidery
Lucy A. Rousselet, embroidery
Maria Jane Salter, painting
Lucy Seaward, embroidery (Mourning Scene)
Mary Ann Shapley, embroidery
Sarah Shannon, embroidery
Ann M. C. Sherburne, working muslin
Frances D. W. Sherburne, painting, working muslin
Margaretta Sherburne, working muslin
Sarah A. Shortridge, working muslin
Catharine Stavers, embroidery
Janet Steele, embroidery, painting (Mourning Scene)
Mary Ann Taft, painting

Ann H. Thompson, embroidery
Hannah Upham, embroidery
Caroline G. M. Willard, painting

**Caroline Stevens** (1800–1873)
*Sampler worked: 1808*
*Length: 10 inches*
*Width: 11½ inches*
*Present owner: Moffatt-Ladd House*
At the age of eight Caroline worked her sampler in silk on unbleached linen, rendering simple and straightforward repetitions of numerals and alphabets along with her name, age, and date.

She was the daughter of Capt. Thomas Bell and Mary Gardner Stevens. Caroline married William Dummer Little (1789–1868). He was for several years a merchant and then found employment in the Portsmouth Customs House.[86]

**Mary Noble** (1798–?)
*Sampler worked: circa 1808*
*Length: 23¾ inches*
*Width: 22 inches*
*Present owner: anonymous*
Mary Noble worked her memorial sampler in silk on green linsey-woolsey, incorporating two alphabets and an urn with a weeping willow and rosebushes. A needlework inscription reads: "An affectionate child pays this tribute of respect to the memory of her father who died 19th June 1808. Aet 48." The whole is enclosed within a Greek fret border worked in cross-stitch.[87]

Mary's father was John Noble, whose death was reported in the *New Hampshire Gazette* for June 21, 1808, in which his age was given as being forty-five. He had built his home on Noble's Island in Portsmouth, as did his brothers. Here they established their fish industry and loaded their catch for shipment to other ports.

The verse Mary chose to embroider no doubt reflected her feelings about her father and one can only speculate that she was convinced that undertaking such a sizable needlework project would produce a fitting memorial for a virtuous man. Mary married John Goodwin.[88]

**Eliza Jane Salter** (1792–1878)
*Sampler worked: 1808*
*Length: 20½ inches*
*Width: 14¾ inches*
*Present owner: Jean Sawtelle*
Elegantly worked in silk on green linsey-woolsey, Eliza Jane's sampler features an arcaded border of fruit that encloses first the alphabet in script, which is followed by the inscription:

> Be good dear child and ease your parents
> Care Choose to be wise rather than fair
> Abstain from those who would thy youth
> betray and from the path of virtue never stray.

Next is worked a row of uppercase letters and a band with the following legend:

> Wisdom is the principle thing therefore get wisdom and with all/ Thy gettings get understanding exalt her and she shall pro/mote The she shall bring The to honor when thou dost embrace her.

In the following section Eliza Jane stitched a repetition of the alphabet in queen stitch, below which is her name and AGED 11 MARCH/ 17 1808, enclosed within a circle of tracery. Verses flank her inscription left and right. At the left appears:

> Beauty is a fading flower
> Which blooms only with
> fragrance when united
> with Virtue …
> virtue is a blooming
> flower whose fruit will
> be perfected in immortality.

At the right appears:

> Delightful talk to hear the
> tender thoughts to teach the
> young ideas how to shoot to

pour the fresh instruction
o'er the mind to breathe
the enliv'ning spirit and to
fix the generous purpose in
the glowing breast.

In a final flourish she centered a basket at the base from which a vine of leaves and flowers branch out to fill the remaining empty spaces of the canvas. Her biographer, Harriet Emery of Sanford, Maine, remembered at the age of seventy-six: "I was very fond of play, did not like any kind of work, so they concluded to send me down to Portsmouth to Miss Eliza Salter, to see if she could do anything with me."

Eliza taught alongside her sisters Abigail (1790–1846) and Sarah Anne Salter Holmes (1786–1868) at 53 Pleasant Street in Portsmouth. "All the Misses Salter were nice as they could be," wrote Emery. "Miss Eliza took unbounded pains to make me orderly. It was 'Harriet, sit up straight,' and 'Harriet, walk erect,' and I never shall forget my saying, 'be you?' They were all four [there was, in fact, a fourth Salter sister, Lucy Maria (1788–1860), who remained unmarried] filled with such consternation it frightened me. I never said it again. ... The memory of them is like a benediction; so full of sympathy and kindness, blessed women, every one. They surely must have received their crown in heaven." Eliza died unmarried on June 4, 1878.[89]


**Mary Pearse** (1801–1818)
*1. Sampler worked: 1810*
*Length: 16 inches*
*Width: 8½ inches*
*2. Sampler worked: 1812*
*Length: 8½ inches*
*Width: 8¼ inches*
*Present owner: unknown*
The sampler Mary Pearse worked in 1810 contained three alphabets with the verse "Jesus permit thy gracious name to stand/ As the first efforts of an infants hand" and was decorated at the base with strawberries in a basket and growing on mounds. She dated it July 22 of that year.

Her second sampler, worked in 1812, also contained three alphabets, along with birds, baskets, and strawberries in pots, and the verse "Beauties like princes from their very youth/ Are perfect strangers to the voice of truth."[90]

Mary was the daughter of Capt. Samuel and Sarah Henderson Pearse. Her sister, Hannah, worked a sampler in 1814, which is also recorded in *American Samplers* by Bolton and Coe. Mary's death at the age of seventeen was reported in the *New Hampshire Gazette* of November 13, 1818.

### Elizabeth Parkhurst Spalding (1809–1878)
*Sampler worked: 1810*
*Length: 12½ inches*
*Width: 11½ inches*
*Present owner: John Foster*
Elizabeth worked a simple sampler in silk on unbleached linen. Unadorned except for her name, it includes repetitions of the alphabet in block and script and the numerals 1 to 14.

### Mary Gerrish (1801–?)
*Memorial sampler worked: 1811*
*Length: 19¾ inches*
*Width: 16 inches*
*Present owner: Newington Historical Society*
Working in silk on linen, Mary Gerrish included a number of design elements found in the samplers worked by Henrietta Tuttell (1803), Mary Langdon (1800), Martha Gaines (1804), Abigail Bowles (1804), Sarah Catherine Moffatt Odiorne (1806), and Mary Elizabeth Coffin (1814). They include the working of alphabets and numerals with a crossband of a flame-stitch-like motif that separates the alphabets above from the decorative elements below.

In the lower half of the sampler a memorial shaded by a weeping willow is flanked by a pair of cartouches enclosing a verse entitled PERFECT HAPPINESS at the left and MARY GERRISH/ AGED 10 1811/ FEAR GOD/ HONOR THY PARENTS at the right. The memorial is inscribed at its base: In Memory of Mr. Thomas Patterson Gerrish obid. Feb 27, 1811. This is followed by a verse that stands above a landscaped stitched in green with a tree and a blooming yellow flower.

Mary Gerrish, the daughter of Timothy and Mary Patterson Gerrish, worked the memorial for her brother, who had been born in 1789.

Her sister, Lydia, later worked a memorial for their father, Timothy Gerrish, in about 1815. (See the entry for Lydia Gerrish.) Mary Gerrish does not seem to have married and her date of death is not known.[91]

**Frances Leighton** (1801–1889)
*Sampler worked: 1813*
*Length: 12 inches*
*Width: 11½ inches*
*Present owner: The Brick Store Museum*
Worked in silk on a linen ground, Frances's sampler is similar to one worked by Mary Elizabeth Wentworth. Both girls lived in Eliot, Maine, just across the Piscataqua River. It is embellished with a variety of decorative motifs that include geometrically worked trees, baskets mounded with fruit, and birds holding V-shaped swags.

Frances was the daughter of Frances Usher Parsons (1778-1865) and Gen. Samuel Leighton. She married Benjamin Emerson of Pittsfield, New Hampshire.[92]

**Mary Elizabeth Coffin** (1806–1827)
*Sampler worked: 1814*
*Length: 20½ inches*
*Width: 16¾ inches*
*Present owner: anonymous*
Mary Elizabeth's sampler in silk on unbleached linen includes repetitions of the alphabet and numerals separated in the upper portion of the sampler, like those of Henrietta Tuttell and others, by a crossband of flame stitch.

Below, a basket of rosebuds perched upon a hillock is centered between cartouches containing the alphabet on the left and her signature, MARY ELIZABETH COFFIN AGED 8 1814, on the right. Below these a verse appears flanked by larger renditions of the letters *A*, *B*, *C*, and *D*.

Mary Elizabeth was the daughter of Charles and Mehitable Sheafe Coffin. She died, unmarried, at the age of twenty-one.[93]

**Hannah S. Pearse** (1803–?)
*Sampler worked: circa 1814*
*Length: 17 inches*

*Width: 12½ inches*
*Present owner: unknown*
Hannah worked her sampler with a border of strawberries enclosing three alphabets, the verse "Jesus permit thy gracious name to stand/ As the first efforts of an infants hand," and decorative motifs of a tree, birds, and flowerpots. Her sister, Mary, had already completed two samplers before her, one in 1810 and the other in 1812. Their parents were Capt. Samuel and Sarah Henderson Pearse.[94]

### Adelaide C. Spalding (1805–?)

*Sampler worked: circa 1814*
*Length: 15¾ inches*
*Width: 9½ inches*
*Present owner: Peter Coues*
Stalwartly carrying out her assignment, Adelaide stitched several repetitions of the alphabet and numerals within a simple arcaded border on unbleached linen. She kept added work to a minimum by only signing her name, without including a date or place-name. She was the daughter of Dr. Lyman Spalding, a 1797 Harvard graduate, and Elizabeth Coues. Her sister, Elizabeth Parkhurst Spalding, was two years her senior. Elizabeth became a teacher and is believed to have included needlework in her curriculum.

In 1814 Dr. Lyman moved his family to New York City, where he maintained his practice until 1821. It is possible that Adelaide completed her sampler there.

In the *Foster Genealogy* Adelaide is reported as having authored an account of a visit aboard the U.S. frigate *President* then at anchor in New York harbor and under the command of Commodore Stephen Decatur. Not long afterward, the vessel was captured by the British outside New York harbor after a six-hour struggle that left twenty-four dead and some fifty-five injured. Among the dead was the young Lt. Fitz-Henry Babbitt, who had invited the family on board.

Adelaide married Joseph Foster of Gloucester, Massachusetts, in September 1838 at her family home on the southwest corner of State and Atkinson Streets in Portsmouth.[95]

### Mary Greenleaf Clark (1806–1820)

*Sampler worked: 1815*

*Length: 12 inches*
*Width: 13 inches*
*Present owner: Jean Sawtelle*

Working in silk on linen, Mary completed repetitions of the alphabet and numerals along with a memorial to the Rev. Joseph Buckminster when she was just eight years old. Ironically, her father died in the same year she worked this memorial.

Mary inscribed the memorial: "In Memory of Rev. Joseph/ Buckminster, D.D./ Pastor of a Church in Portsmouth/ NH who died suddenly/ in this vicinity while on a/ journey for health June 10,/ 1812 ae 61." In addition, she stitched a basket with flowers and the verse:

> O ever honoured ever dear adieu
> How many tender names are lost in you
> Keep safe O tomb thy precious sacred trust
> Till Life divine awake his Sleeping dust.

Mary was the daughter of Enoch Moody and Mary Woodward Clark, who died on March 25, 1820, after a lingering illness, leaving her thirteen-year-old daughter. It is interesting to note that her father, Enock Moody Clark, was a teacher in the academy started by the Rev. Timothy Alden in 1801.[96]

**Sarah Fitzgerald** (1807–1842)
*Sampler worked: circa 1815*
*Length: 17 inches*
*Width: 17 inches*
*Present owner: unknown*

According to Ethel Bolton and Eva Coe, Sarah's memorial sampler included a vine and cloverleaf border enclosing two alphabets and the needlework inscription: "Sacred to the Memory of Mrs. A. Fitzgerald. In memory of an affectionate mother, who died March 1st 1808, aged 40 years. Wrought by her daughter Sarah Fitzgerald under inspection of Mary E. Hill." The memorial inscription is embellished with weeping willows, small trees, a dog, birds, and a large basket of flowers, all set out on a green base.

Sarah also worked a verse entitled "The Death Of The Righteous," which had been printed in *The Clergyman's Almanac* for 1814, and decorated it with baskets of fruit and a spray of flowers with a bird.[97]

The records of North Church of Portsmouth reveal the death, from consumption, of Mrs. A. Fitzgerald on March 3, 1809, at age thirty-nine. The same records contain the report of Sarah's baptism on April 10, 1808, as the daughter of Richard and Abigail Fitzgerald.[98] She died at the age of thirty-five in 1842, unmarried.[99]

**Lydia Gerrish** (dates unknown)
*Mourning picture worked: after 1815*
*Length: 17¾ inches*
*Width: 20⅜ inches*
*Present owner: New Hampshire Historical Society*
Worked in silk and watercolor on silk, a female figure stands before a weeping willow tree at a monument with her arm outstretched. A printed legend on the monument proclaims: TO THE MEMORY/ OF/ TIMOTHY GERRISH/ OBT. DEC. 30, 1815, AET. 60. The glass mat bears the inscription: BY LYDIA GERRISH.[100]

Timothy Gerrish (1755–1815) was the eldest son of Capt. Timothy and Joanna Cutts Gerrish. He married Mary Patterson and served for many years as sheriff of Rockingham County.[101]

Lydia married John Dodge of Exeter, New Hampshire, on September 1, 1816, and probably made her mourning picture before her marriage.[102]

**Sarah Jane Wentworth** (1807–1841)
*Sampler worked: 1816*
*Length: 15½ inches*
*Width: 12 inches*
*Present owner: Elvira F. Bass*
This simple sampler worked on unbleached linen includes repetitions of the alphabet and numerals followed by her signature, SARAH JANE WENTWORTH AGED/ 9 YEARS OCTOBER THE 30 1816. This is followed by two lines of verse extolling the virtues of industry, all enclosed within a sawtooth border.

Sarah Jane was the daughter of Joshua (1785–1816) and Ann Tredick Wentworth. On November 17, 1829, she married Capt. William Parker. The couple had five children. Sarah Jane died in Portsmouth on September 27, 1841.

**Hannah Langdon** (1805–1839)
*Sampler worked: 1817*
*Length: 17¾ inches*
*Width: 12¾ inches*
*Present owner: Jean Sawtelle*

In silk on unbleached linen Hannah worked repetitions of the alphabet followed by the inscription, WROUGHT BY HANNAH/ LANGDON PORTSMOUTH/ NEW HAMPSHIRE OCTOBER 14. A lozenge shape within which AGED 12 is stitched centers the base and is flanked by four trees, some of which still show the inking of the forms to be stitched.

Hannah Langdon was the daughter of Rev. Joseph Langdon and Patience Pickering of Newington, New Hampshire. She was the sister of Elizabeth Langdon, who worked a sampler in 1805. She married Samuel Langdon in 1832 and they had two sons and a daughter, John, Joseph, and Harriet.

**Mary Cate** (1809–?)
*Memorial sampler worked: 1818–1819*
*Length: 23½ inches*
*Width: 17 inches*
*Present owner: anonymous*

Mary Cate worked a unique memorial sampler on green linsey-woolsey that she dedicated to the memory of William Cate, who may have been her grandfather or perhaps her uncle. A border of symmetrical design is composed of a basket of flowers centering the top, flanked by vines and roses adorned with bowed ribbons. Below these, at either side, stand a pair of obelisk forms entwined with foliage and bearing memorial inscriptions. While the inscription on the obelisk at left is obscured because of fabric loss, the one at right reads, SACRED TO THE/ MEMORY OF MR./ WILLIAM CATE/ WHO DIED 1817/ AND MRS. DEBORA/H CATE WHO DI/ED A.D. 1818. Centering the bottom is an open book of verse that rests upon a lyre and another stringed instrument.

Within this stylish border Mary stitched a verse followed by repetitions of the alphabet rendered in a much more florid style than most other Portsmouth samplers. Each band of alphabets is separated from the next by a line of cross-stitch. Below these she stitched WROUGHT BY MARY CATE IN THE 9TH YEAR OF/ HER AGE AD 1818. She then stitched the names of her parents; birth dates and places and the

*Sampler worked by Mary Cate in 1818–19. Courtesy of Sotheby Parke Bernet Inc., New York.*

date of their marriage; followed by the names and birth dates of her three brothers, Samuel, James, and George.

Mary was the daughter of Samuel Cate (born in Portsmouth in 1785) and Mary Stacy Cate (born in Marblehead in 1785). Her brothers were Samuel, born in 1812; James, born in 1813; and George, born in 1816. In 1837 she was married by Elder David Millard of the Portsmouth Central Baptist Church to James Garland.[103] Records of the church dated March 14, 1840, include an entry that tells us that they "had a Church Meeting in the afternoon & evening & Brs James Garland, Jehoiwhin Decoff & Sisters Elizabeth Nutter, Frances Akerman, Henrietta Willey, Lucy F. Willey, Nancy Demutt, Mary Garland told what great things the Lord had done for their Souls & were recd for the Ordinancy of Baptism."[104]

### Elizabeth Lake (1805–1843)
*Sampler worked: 1817*
*Dimensions: unknown*
*Present owner: Portsmouth Historical Society*
Elizabeth worked in silk on green linsey-woolsey. She included four alphabets and one set of numerals in the upper portion of her sampler along with a row of orbs set into a sawtooth band. Below this she signed her work: ELIZABETH LAKE AE 12 PORTSMOUTH 1817.

The remainder of the sampler is devoted to the depiction of a scene with a large Georgian-style house, trees, people, and birds. The house strongly resembles the Moffatt-Ladd House on Market Street in Portsmouth, as well as the house at the corner of Austin and Summer Streets, where Elizabeth lived. Set above the trees flanking the house are the verses: "Tis education/ forms the common/ mind/ Just as the/twig is bent/ the tree's inclined" and "Modesty is a/ quality that highly/ adorns a young lady."

Elizabeth was the daughter of John and Hannah Salter Lake and the wife of Rufus Hubbard, whom she married in 1826.[105] Her mother was the daughter of Capt. Titus Salter (1745–1775), a grantee of the town of Success, New Hampshire.[106]

*Sampler worked by Caroline Vaughan in 1818. Courtesy of the Baltimore Museum of Art.*

**Mary Catherine Evans** (1806–?)
*Sampler worked: 1818*
*Length: 17 inches*
*Width: 17 inches*
*Present owner: Jean Sawtelle*
Worked in silk on unbleached linen, the upper two-thirds of Mary's sampler is composed of bands of the alphabet and numerals. The lower section encloses verse 515, "Jesus permit thy gracious name," within a sawtooth broder along with MARY CATHERINE EVANS AGED 12 1818 PORTSMOUTH NH. The familiar horizontally banded geometric baskets containing flowers flank the inscription and legend.

Mary Catherine married James B. Pray. They had one son, Isaac Mead Pray, and two daughters, Elizabeth B. Pray and Helen Dunbar Pray.

**Elizabeth Fernald** (1807–1821)
*Sampler worked: 1818*
*Length: 17 inches*
*Width: 12 inches*
*Present owner: Jean Sawtelle*
Worked in silk on green linsey-woolsey Elizabeth's sampler contains bands of the alphabet and numerals followed by the legend:

> Be good dear child and ease your
> Parents care choose rather to be wise
> Than fair abstain from those who would
> Thy youth betray and from the path of
> Virtue never stray.

The lower portion of the sampler centers her name, ELIZABETH FERNALD/ AGED 11 1818/ PORTSMOUTH NH, and is decorated by flanking birds and baskets of flowers.

Baptized in Portsmouth on January 25, 1807, she was the daughter of Nathaniel Weeks Fernald and Elizabeth Melcher Fernald.[107] Nathaniel operated a tailor shop at the east end of State Street. The elder Elizabeth died two years later, in 1809, of consumption and in 1821 the younger Elizabeth succumbed to the same illness. She was fourteen years and nine months old.[108]

*Imprint from the woodblock used to make a silk memorial to John Badger in 1831. Woodblock in the collections of the Old York Historical Society, York, Maine.*

IN MEMORY OF
JOHN BADGER,
Who died February 9, 1831,
AGED 53 YEARS,
In Portsmouth, N. H.

Happy the man who lives by nature's laws
And dies in peace and quietness.

*Printed silk memorial to John Badger made in 1831. Collections of Portsmouth Historical Society. Dan Gair photograph.*

**Elmira Sullivan** (1808–1877)
*Sampler worked: 1818*
*Length: 15 inches*
*Width: 12 inches*
*Present owner: unknown*
Elmira Sullivan stitched her sampler when she was ten years old and worked three alphabets and the verse "Youth is time to improve," to which Bolton and Coe assigned number 601.

She was the daughter of Capt. John and Mary Sullivan. She married Ammi R. H. Fernald of Boston on December 23, 1832, and had four daughters.[109]


**Caroline Vaughan** (1808–1849)
*Sampler worked: 1818*
*Length: $16\frac{3}{4}$ inches*
*Width: 19 inches*
*Present owner: Baltimore Museum of Art*
Caroline worked her sampler in silk on green linsey-woolsey while she was a student in the Mary Walden School in Portsmouth. She included the usual repetitions of the alphabet and numerals at the top of her sampler. At the center is the verse "Jesus permit thy gracious name to stand," flanked by a mirror image pair of flower-laden baskets. Below them a pair of angels flank a banner of cross-stitched florets.

The balance of the sampler is filled out with the cross-stitched Portsmouth motif of a house and barn connected by a fence and embellished with a birdhouse, birds, and trees. At the base she signed her work CAROLINE VAUGHAN AGED 10 WORKED AT MARY WALDENS SCHOOL OCTOBER 28 1818. An arcaded border encloses the main body of her needlework.

Caroline was the daughter of Michael and Mary Vaughan. According to the *Portsmouth Directory* of 1839–40, she worked at tailoring at 67 State Street and lived at 75 Water Street. She died on July 1, 1849.[110]


**Priscilla Hall Badger** (1804–1842)
*Sampler worked: 1818*
*Length: 17 inches*
*Width: $21\frac{1}{2}$ inches*

*Present owner: Dr. and Mrs. Edward Jackson*

Worked in silk on green linsey-woolsey six months prior to the sampler done by Caroline Vaughan, Priscilla's is nearly identical even though it was worked at another school, the one operated by Elizabeth S. Smith.

She worked the same alphabets and flower baskets along with the same pair of angels. Here the verse "How blest the maid whom circling years improve" stands in place of the one chosen by Caroline. Below, Priscilla has rendered an even more elaborate version of the Portsmouth scene with five trees rather than the three worked by Caroline. She signed her work PRISCILLA HALL BADGER AGED 13 WORKED AT ELIZABETH S. SMITH'S SCHOOL PORTSMOUTH APRIL 28TH 1818. Once again, a variant of an arcaded border encloses the whole needlework.

The daughter of John and Elizabeth Peirce Stanwood Badger, she was born on November 16, 1804. Priscilla married Col. Brackett Hutchins, a Portsmouth druggist and apothecary, on April 24, 1831. A printed silk memorial in the collections of the Portsmouth Historical Society was probably ordered shortly after her father's death, just two months before Priscilla married.[111]

**Deborah Laighton** (dates unknown)

*Sampler worked: 1818 or 1819*
*Length: 17½ inches*
*Width: 23¼ inches*
*Present owner: unknown*

Deborah worked her sampler in silk on linsey-woolsey under the watchful eye of Mary Ann Smith. Her work closely resembles the work done by Priscilla Hall Badger in that she executed the same alphabets, verse, baskets of flowers, and a red-roofed house with a barn in a shade of gold. Between the house and barn are the same number and form of trees seen in the Badger example and above it all a pair of angels hold a sawtooth banner punctuated by flowers. She signed the sampler DEBORAH LAIGHTON WORKED AT MARY ANN SMITH'S SCHOOL PORTSMOUTH OCTOBER 15 181(8 or 9). In both cases the girls used exactly the same border motif. The strength of the similarities found in the samplers worked by Deborah Laighton and Priscilla Hall Badger clearly demonstrates that Elizabeth S. and Mary Ann Smith shared common space in which to hold classes for their students and more than likely worked together.

Deborah was the twelfth child of Luke Mills Laighton (1766–1834) and Elizabeth Mendum Laighton (1767–1854). She was named after her older sister, Deborah, who had been a student at Rev. Timothy Alden's academy, and had died in 1803. There are no records of Deborah Laighton's marriage or death.[112]

**Sarah A. Bailey** (1814–?)
*Sampler worked: 1820*
*Length: 18 inches*
*Width: 7¾ inches*
*Present owner: Strawbery Banke Museum*
Sarah was just six years old when she worked this simple, straightforward sampler of alphabets and numerals in silk on unbleached linen, signing it, SARAH A. BAILEY/ AGED 6 1820.

Sarah Aba Bailey was one of five children born to Martha and Thomas Darling Bailey. On February 18, 1833, she married Elias Taft Aldrich and on November 11, 1836, brought a son named Thomas Bailey Aldrich into the world. Thomas went on to become one of the nineteenth century's most notable American authors. In addition, he would become the highly respected editor of the *Atlantic Monthly*.[113]

**Caroline Odiorne** (1805–?)
*Sampler worked: 1820*
*Length: 12½ inches*
*Width: 7⅝ inches*
*Present owner: Jean Sawtelle*
Caroline worked her band sampler with repetitions of the alphabet and numerals. She stitched the verse:

> Love the Lord and he
> will be a tender Father unto thee.
> Caroline Odi
> orn Aged 14 July 1820

Caroline was the eldest daughter of George Beck Odiorne, who was a cordwainer by trade.[114] He lived in Portsmouth, New Hampshire. She married Samuel Ham, Jr. of New Castle, New Hampshire.

**Eliza J. Bennett** (1810–1844)
*Sampler worked: 1820*
*Length: 16 inches*
*Width: 12 inches*
*Present owner: Mrs. Jeremy Waldron*
Eliza worked her sampler on unbleached linen, including several repetitions of the alphabet along with numerals. These are separated by six crossbands worked in various designs. Nearly half of the sampler is occupied by a verse to which she appended her name, ELIZA J. BENNETT.

Eliza was born in Portsmouth, the daughter of John and Jane Bennett,[115] and in 1835 married Stacy Hall Jr. of New York.[116] Prior to her marriage she was the assistant at the First Female School in Portsmouth in 1827 and in 1834 is recorded as a teacher in the Portsmouth public schools.[117, 118]

**Mary Harvey** (1810–1849)
*Sampler worked: 1821*
*Length: $16\frac{1}{2}$ inches*
*Width: 17 inches*
*Present owner: Portsmouth Historical Society*
A simple arcaded border punctuated by treelike forms encloses three alphabets and the verse "How blest the maid whom circling years improve," all rendered in silk on unbleached linen.

Mary Harvey was the daughter of Mary Bell of New Castle, New Hampshire, and Caleb Harvey of Portsmouth, a carpenter. She married Capt. Ames B. Gunnison of Portsmouth and had two children, Maud and Nathaniel. According to tradition, the sampler was given to the Portsmouth Historical Society by their grandchildren, Andrew Caswell and Minnie Caswell Fowle.[119, 120]

**Ann Simes Jones** (1813–1891)
*Sampler worked: 1821*
*Length: $17\frac{1}{2}$ inches*
*Width: $12\frac{1}{2}$ inches*
*Present owner: anonymous*
In a very simply rendered piece of needlework of silk on linen, Ann made a sampler that includes several repetitions of the alphabet along with the verse, "Teach me to feel anothers woe/ To hide the

*Sampler worked by Margaret Lowd in 1822. Courtesy of the Baltimore Museum of Art.*

faults that I to/ Others show that/ Mercy show to me," and signed it
ANN S. JONES/ AGED 7/ 1821.

   She was the daughter of Ann Parry Jones, who worked a silk
memorial to her father in 1801 (included in this survey), and William
Jones of Portsmouth. Ann married Parry Lunt of Philadelphia on
October 28, 1834. She later remarried after Lunt's death, this time to
Mark H. Wentworth, on February 7, 1856.[122]


**Anzolette Hussey** (1812–1895)
*Two samplers worked: 1821*
*1. Length: 15$\frac{3}{4}$ inches*
*Width: 17$\frac{1}{2}$ inches*
*2. Length: 13$\frac{1}{8}$ inches*
*Width: 10 inches*
*Present owner: Smithsonian Institution, Bequest of Mrs. Abby Knight
McLane*

Anzolette Hussey worked two samplers, both in 1821. Each appears
to have been worked at a different school, since their styles vary and
the grounds are also different. The first was worked on an
unbleached linen ground in silk threads. Enclosed within an arcaded
border with alternating flower blossoms Anzolette worked repetitions
of the alphabet and numerals. Below these a basket filled with flowers and set upon a plinth of cross-stitch in various colors is centered
between lozenges that contain the inscriptions ANZOLETTE/ HUSSEY/
AGED 9 at left and IN THE YEAR OF/ OUR LORD/ 1821 at the right. Each
inscription is festooned within the lozenge with a tasseled garland.

   Her second sampler was worked on green linsey-woolsey in silk
threads. Within a meandering band punctuated by alternating small
star shapes, she worked four repetitions of the alphabet along with
numerals. The bottom section of the sampler is decorated with a centered pair of trees rendered in simple geometric form, each of which
has a single bird perched at the top. These are flanked by baskets
holding blossoms, all worked in geometric shapes.

   Anzolette was the daughter of Captain Andrew Hussey (1783-
1861) and married Ebenezer Knight in 1835. They had one child,
Mary Anzollette, who died in 1851 at the age of fifteen. Anzollette had
been a student in the First Female School of Portsmouth in 1827
when she was fourteen years old.[123]

**Sarah L. Whidden** (1812–?)
*Sampler worked: 1822*
*Length: 9¾ inches*
*Width: 6¾ inches*
*Present owner: Newington Historical Society*
Sarah L. Whidden, sister of Mary Ann and Frances Whidden, wrought a sampler with Portsmouth, New Hampshire, embroidered on it.

Sarah L. Whidden married Reuel G. Bean of Boston in 1834. The couple had one child, who died in infancy.

**Margaret Lowd** (1812–1824)
*Sampler worked: 1822*
*Length: 19¼ inches*
*Width: 15¾ inches*
*Present owner: Baltimore Museum of Art*
Working in the distinctive silk on green linsey-woolsey, Margaret created a flower and leaf border that encloses four alphabets and the numerals along with the inscription MARGARET LOWD WORKED THIS SAMPLER AGED 10 YEARS 1822. The lower portion of her needlework is decorated with the familiar Portsmouth house, which she chose to render in diminutive proportions in comparison with the houses on other students' samplers. The house and the adjacent barn are separated by a fence and flanked by a trio of trees and a birdhouse.

The March 23, 1824, edition of the *Portsmouth Journal* carried the announcement of Margaret's death at the age of twelve. Her father was Hunking Lowd, a cooper with a shop on Bow Street. The family lived on Anthony Street.[124]

**Adaline M. Ferguson** (1809–?)
*Sampler worked: 1822*
*Length: 16 inches*
*Width: 17¾ inches*
*Present owner: Betty Ring*
Adaline used silk on green linsey-woolsey to stitch a familiar arcaded border interwoven with a leaf that encloses repetitions of the alphabet and the verse, "Jesus permit they gracious Name to stand." These are flanked by a pair of generously filled flower baskets similar to those found in the work of other Portsmouth students working at the

same time. Below, the ever-vigilant pair of angels holding their banner aloft make yet another appearance. They float above a rendition of the house, fence, birdhouse, and barn motif. Adaline worked three trees into her scene and decorated each with a bird perched in its branches. At one end of the fence a large bird stands watch. At the other, a four-legged animal gingerly treads its way along—perhaps the family cat.

Little is known about Adaline other than the information she recorded about herself on her sampler. Her father may have been James Ferguson, a joiner whose name is found in the 1821 and 1827 Portsmouth Directories. He is known to have worked with James Nutter on the Portsmouth Academy building. In 1839 the *Portsmouth Gazette* reported James Ferguson's death in Eliot, Maine, having been "formerly of Portsmouth."[125]

**Elizabeth Dore** (1809–1864)
*Sampler worked: 1822*
*Length: 17¼ inches*
*Width: 15½ inches*
*Present owner: Mary Jaene Edmonds*
Worked in silk on linen, Elizabeth's sampler includes four repetitions of the alphabet along with three repetitions of numerals. Below them she placed two sets of verse opposite one another, one headed "Extract" and the other "Three Golden Rules." A cluster of grapes together with a leaf decorate the space between the verses. The lower portion of her sampler is embellished with a double-chimney house, a fence standing before three trees, a birdhouse, and a barn. At the bottom is the legend ELIZABETH DORE AGED 13 PORTSMOUTH MAY 31 A.D. 1822. The entire needlework is enclosed within an arcaded border entwined with a strawberry or leaf motif.

Elizabeth was the daughter of John and Elizabeth Dore, who lived on Ham Street in Portsmouth. She married Ezekiel Dyer, the son of a mariner, in 1829. In 1832 Ezekiel's death at the age of twenty-five was reported in the *Portsmouth Journal* and Elizabeth seems to have gone to live with her widowed mother in a house on Bridge Street. Elizabeth died, at the age of fifty-five, on March 17, 1864.[126]

**Lucy Maria Wiggin** (1815–1889)
*Sampler worked: 1822*
*Length: 15½ inches*
*Width: 18½ inches*
*Present owner: Strawbery Banke Museum*
Lucy worked in silk on green linsey-woolsey to stitch the alphabet and
numerals before moving on to the verse, "How blest the maid whom circling years improve," which is flanked by sprays of blossoming
branches. Below is the familiar Portsmouth scene composed of a double-
chimney house, a fence standing before a pair of trees, a birdhouse, and
a barn. A pair of baskets mounded with round fruit are placed either
side of the scene and below she stitched the legend LUCY MARIA WIGGIN
AGED 7 YEARS PORTSMOUTH NEW HAMPSHIRE. Lucy is the only one of the
students stitching this scene to have included the state name and the
city name in her work. She worked a sawtooth border intertwined with
triangular shapes representing a blossom with leaves.

Lucy Maria was born in Stratham, New Hampshire, on March
18, 1815, the daughter of Joseph and Rhoda Sinclair Wiggin. She was
a teacher in Portsmouth in the summer classes given at the 1834
Female Public School, and in 1838 married Calvin Hodgdon. The couple lived in Exeter, New Hampshire, and had four children.[127]

**Mary Elizabeth Senter** (1808–1894)
*Sampler worked: circa 1822*
*Dimensions: unknown*
*Present owner: unknown*
Mary Elizabeth worked a classic Portsmouth sampler on unbleached
linen. Within an arcaded border she worked several repetitions of the
alphabet and numerals, below which she placed a verse on virtue
flanked by a pair of flower-laden baskets. At the base of her sampler
stand a house at the left and barn at the right separated by five trees
bearing birds and set behind a fence. She inscribed it, MARY ELIZA-
BETH SENTER AGED 14.

She was the daughter of William and Dorothy Senter, who
married in 1808. William was active in the well-established firm of
Judkins and Senter, which produced some of the most fashionable furniture available in the city.

Mary became a mantua maker and later a dressmaker. She
married Daniel Senter in 1842 and died in 1894.[128]

**Elizabeth Moses Tucker** (1812–1889)
*Sampler worked: 1823*
*Length: 6¼ inches*
*Width: 14 inches*
*Present owner: anonymous*
Done in silk on unbleached linen, this marking sampler was worked in a simple and direct form with no embellishments at all. Elizabeth chose to complete the repetitions of the alphabet, sign her work, and move on to other things!

She was the daughter of Michael W. Tucker, a Rye farmer, and her mother was Elizabeth Moses Tucker, who had lived in Portsmouth. Elizabeth married Nathaniel Balch, who worked on the farm of John L. Elwyn on Rye Road in Portsmouth, in 1835. They had two sons and one daughter.[129]

**Frances M. Tuckerman** (1814–?)
*Sampler worked: circa 1823*
*Dimensions: unknown*
*Present owner: Mrs. Phillips Masco*
In silk on linen Frances worked several repetitions of the alphabet and numerals in the upper half of her sampler. The lower half she reserved for the working of an exuberant version of the Portsmouth scene with a pair of cherubs holding aloft a double swag with tassels, a verse enclosed within each. Flanking the cherubs and their swags are a pair of baskets filled with a variety of blossoms. Below all of this one sees the traditional scene of house, fence, and barn with birdhouse nearby. At least seven birds populate the seven trees and perching spaces. Within a cross-stitched border she signed her work and dated it. The whole is enclosed in an arcaded border of blossoms or strawberries, much as the sampler made by Elizabeth Dore.

Some four years later Frances, then thirteen, would be counted among the students attending the "First Female School in Portsmouth, N.H." She was the daughter of Capt. William Tuckerman, a packetmaster, of Portsmouth. In December 1835 she married James W. Emery, a New York merchant.[130]

**Lucretia Jones Trefethen** (1813–1892)
*Sampler worked: 1824*
*Length: 19½ inches*
*Width: 16¼ inches*
*Present owner: Private Owner*
Lucretia worked three complete repetitions of the alphabet as well as the numerals in silk on linen. Also included is this verse:

> O may virtue forever afford you protection
> Inculcate your precepts and guide you in truth
> May your heart be the seat of no baneful affection
> To embitter in age or to sully in youth.

She decorated the needlework with sprays of white blossoms placed at either side of the verse. Below the sprays and flanking an hourglass-shaped cartouche with her name are a pair of baskets holding yet more sprays of white-blossomed flowers.

Lucretia married Archibald A. Peterson. She died on May 29, 1892.[131]

**Lydia Chadbourne** (1813–?)
*Sampler worked: 1824*
*Dimensions: unknown*
*Present owner: Strawbery Banke Museum*
Worked in silk on linen and enclosed within a sawtooth border, Lydia stitched repetitions of the alphabet and numerals along with the inscription LYDIA CHADBOURNE AGED/ 11 YEARS 1824 and the verse:

> I know then this truth enough for man to know
> Virtue above is happiness below.

She was the daughter of James and Susan McIntyre Chadbourne of Berwick, Maine. She never married. In 1831 her sister, Elizabeth, also worked a sampler.[132]

**Mary A. Reding** (1815–?)
*Sampler worked: 1824*
*Length: 14½ inches*

*Width: 13½ inches*
*Present owner: Betty Ring*
In silk on linen, within a border of pink cabbage roses, Mary worked
repetitions of the alphabet and numerals along with a verse exclaim-
ing, "Time well employed is a most certain gain." Below her exercises
of alphabets and numerals she fashioned a picture, in tent stitch, with
at least four houses nestled within a landscape of trees, clouds, and
water. Mary's work, as needlework scholar Betty Ring points out, is
strongly reminiscent of samplers commonly done in Portland, Maine.
Her sister, Harriet, worked a very similar sampler in about 1826.
Mary Ann was the daughter of Charles and Phebe Reding of
Portsmouth. Her father was a rope maker.[133]

## Sophia Jane B. Johnson (1817–1856)
*Sampler worked: 1824*
*Length: 19¾ inches*
*Width: 16½ inches*
*Present owner: unknown*
Sophia Jane B. Johnson worked three alphabets above a pious verse
flanked by flower baskets and also flanked by winged angels above a
house and barn with birds and flower baskets over an inscription ,
SOPHIA JANE B. JOHNSON AGE 7 1824 PORTSMOUTH, N.H. All are
enclosed in a stylized flower and vine border.

Sophia Jane, daughter of Brackett and Sarah J. Johnson, was a
student at the First Female School in Portsmouth, New Hampshire,
March 1, 1827.

Sophia J. Johnson operated a private school on Hanover Street
in 1839, according to the *Portsmouth Directory* for 1839.

## Sarah Wheeler (dates unknown)
*Sampler worked: circa 1824*
*Length: 17¼ inches*
*Width: 17¼ inches*
*Present owner: Warner House Association*
In a fashion similar to that of Mary Ann Reding and worked in silk on
linen, Sarah stitched a border of pink and white roses and completed
repetitions of the alphabet and numerals. She decorated the lower

portion of her sampler with a pair of large houses between which a small spray of flowers and her name appear.

She was probably the daughter of Hunking Wheeler, a trader with a store on Ceres Street. His name is found in the *Portsmouth City Directory* from 1821 through 1829; in the 1810 census of New Hampshire, only one such Hunking Wheeler appears in Portsmouth.

**Ann Eliza Damrell** (1817–?)
*Sampler worked: 1825*
*Length: 11 inches*
*Width: 8 inches*
*Present owner: Strawbery Banke Museum*
Working in silk on linen, Ann Eliza made a very straightforward sampler framed within a hemstitch border on three sides and a sawtooth crossband at the bottom. Three repetitions of the alphabet and one set of numerals are followed by her name stitched as ANN ELIZA DAMRELL AD 8 and four lines of verse.

She was the daughter of Capt. William Damrell. Her mother's name does not appear in records we have seen. She was a student in the First Female School in Portsmouth and her name appears on the roster printed in March 1829. On September 5, 1842, she married John S. Dodge of Greenland, New Hampshire.[134]

**Almira Hilton** (dates unknown)
*Sampler worked: 1825*
*Length: 11½ inches*
*Width: 10½ inches*
*Present owner: Jean Sawtelle*
The very plain sampler, worked in silk on unbleached linen, includes repetitions of the alphabet and numerals along with the young student's name and age at the base, ALMIRA HILTON/ AGED 14 YEARS/ PORTSMOUTH JUNE 14 1825. Curiously for this late date, a half crown appears just above and to the left of her name.

A search of genealogical information available on the numerous branches of the Hilton family on the seacoast have not yet produced an Almira.

**Harriet Ann Dockum** (1816–1840)
*Sampler worked: 1825*
*Length: 25½ inches*
*Width: 21 inches*
*Present owner: Jean Sawtelle*

Harriet Dockum worked her sampler in silk on linen. She created a border of linked lozenge shapes, a design that matches the one worked by Harriet Biron Reding in 1826 and Ann Mary Gerrish some six years later. The teacher of the three girls seems to have focused strong attention on the depiction of buildings as well. Each of the three samplers includes one or more structures as an important element of the overall scene.

Harriet Dockum included, as one expects, repetitions of the alphabet and numerals in the upper half of her sampler. The lower portion is given over to the rendering of the widely used verse "Jesus permit thy gracious name." The verse is flanked by a pair of flower-filled baskets, above which appear a second pair of baskets filled with mounded fruit.

The balance of her sampler is filled with an ambitious rendering of what appears to be a three-story public building with a central tower. At its left and right appear trees depicted in a highly geometric form such as those seen in the work of Ann Mary Gerrish (1832) and Elizabeth Fabyan Willey (1834). Just outside the flanking trees are a pair of two-story dwellings with hip roofs. The entire lower scene of buildings and trees is set behind a fence with a central arched opening. She signed the sampler HARRIET ANN DOCKUM AGED 10 YEARS. OCTOBER 22 1825.

Harriet was the daughter of Samuel M. and Lucy M. Dockum. Samuel was a Portsmouth cabinetmaker. She married Dr. John T. G. Pike of Exeter, New Hampshire, and their portraits now hang in the John Paul Jones House in Portsmouth. They had one daughter, Mary Frances, before Harriet died in 1840 at the age of twenty-four.[135]

**Harriet Biron Reding** (dates unknown)
*Sampler worked: circa 1826*
*Length: 16½ inches*
*Width: 12 inches*
*Present owner: Betty Ring*

Stitched in silk on linen, Harriet worked an uncommon ring border, though one that is also to be found in the work of Ann Gerrish.

She was the sister of Mary Ann Reding and married John M. White of Boston on April 28, 1836.[136]

**Mary L. Starbird** (1814–?)
*Sampler worked: 1825*
*Length: 16 inches*
*Width: 21½ inches*
*Present owner: Strawbery Banke Museum*
Worked on unbleached linen and enclosed within an exuberant border like the one found on the samplers worked by Harriet Reding (1826) and Ann M. Gerrish (1832), Mary worked repetitions of the alphabet and numerals. Centering a tablet with a sawtooth border, Mary stitched a verse entitled "Conscience" and then added MARY L. STARBIRD'S SAMPLER/ WROUGHT IN THE 11TH YEAR OF HER AGE./ AT E. M. ROBINSON'S SCHOOL/ PORTSMOUTH OCTOBER 14TH 1825.

The decoration of the lower portion of the sampler includes other birds, sprigs of flowers, a central container with flowering branches and a catlike animal along with a dromedary. At the base, sitting upon a green stitched ground, are a pair of three-story houses with two chinmeys which are separated by a fence behind which we see four trees with three birds.

E. M. Robinson is believed to have been Emeline Robinson, who taught school in 1825 at the Plains in Portsmouth. There was a long tradition of Starbirds residing in Dover and Durham, New Hampshire. It is probable that Mary came to Portsmouth to be educated.

**Caroline B. Sherburne** (1816–?)
*Sampler worked: 1825*
*Length: 26 inches*
*Width: 8¼ inches*
*Present owner: Wanetta Bartholomew*
The inscription on this sampler reads CAROLINE B. SHERBURNE WROUGHT IN THE 9TH YEAR OF HER AGE, PORTSMOUTH, OCTOBER 21, 1825.

The sampler was stitched in silk on linen. At the base is a three-story brick house with two chinmeys, then a fence with geometrically shaped trees, above which a large bird is nesting. A flower basket appears on the left side of the sampler above the brick house.

Caroline B. Sherburne married Rufus Amazeen of New Castle, New Hampshire, in 1837.[137]

**Sarah Jane Folsom** (1817–1836)
*Sampler worked: 1826*
*Length: 20¼ inches*
*Width: 16½ inches*
*Present owner: Portsmouth Historical Society*
Sarah worked repetitions of the alphabet and numerals along with a lengthy verse in silk on linen. Next to the verse she worked a large banded basket in a herringbone pattern that she filled with flowers. At the bottom of her sampler she stitched a pair of smaller baskets that flank her name, age, and the date.

Sarah was the daughter of Nathaniel and Mary Smith Folsom. She died at the age of nineteen in 1836. A sampler worked by her sister, Mary Frances, in 1835 is also preserved in the same collection.[138]

**Ann Elizabeth Ham** (1815–1899)
*Sampler worked: 1826*
*Length: 19½ inches*
*Width: 26½ inches*
*Present owner: Jean Sawtelle*
Six repetitions of the alphabet are set out in silk on linen followed by two verses of poetry entitled "The Grave." The verses are flanked by pairs of baskets with mounded fruit, the baskets rendered in two different sizes. This is followed by a pair of angels holding a banner aloft with baskets of flowers at right and left.

The scene at the base of Ann's sampler includes yet two more baskets brimming with flowers. There is also the familiar Portsmouth landscape composed here of a house, fence, four trees, a barn, birds, and a dog. It is inscribed ANN ELIZABETH HAM AGED 11 PORTSMOUTH NEW HAMPSHIRE MARKED AT MISS ANN L. C. JONES 1826. An arcaded border of flower or strawberry blossoms frames her needlework.

Ann L. C. Jones was the daughter of William Jones. In December 1826 she married William J. Southerin, a West Indies goods and provisions store owner in Portsmouth. They had two children, both of whom died before reaching the age of sixteen months.

Ann Elizabeth Ham was the daughter of William Ham, a Portsmouth merchant, and Ann Nancy Green Ham. They were married in 1797. She was one of three children. In 1836 she married Allen Treat, a stonecutter in Portsmouth. They had eight children.[139]

**Emily Furber** (1817–?)
*Sampler worked: 1827*
*Length: 25½ inches*
*Width: 23 inches*
*Present owner: Rita F. Conant*
In silk on linen Emily worked repetitions of the alphabet and numerals above a pair of couplets enclosed within swagged garlands held aloft by cherubs at either side. Flanking them are rounded baskets with handles, each filled with flowers and blossoms. Below this scene she stitched the verse, "Jesus permit the gracious name to stand," identified in Bolton and Coe's *American Samplers* as number 515 in their lexicon of verses.

Filling the bottom portion of her sampler is a basket with a variety of blossoming flowers. The body of the basket is decorated in diamond shapes of alternating blue and white. The handles spread out at the sides like ribbons curving away from the basket's rim. At the left of the basket decoration is the rendering of the Portsmouth scene in something of a miniaturized version. All the same familiar elements of house, fence, trees with birds, birdhouse, barn, and dog are present.

She inscribed the sampler EMILY FURBER HER SAMPLER AGED 10 WORKED MARCH 16 1827. Emily may have been the daughter of Augustus Furber, a joiner who lived on Jefferson Street in Portsmouth, who left for Durham, New Hampshire, sometime before 1839.[140]


**Mary Ann Davis** (1816–?)
*Sampler worked: 1828*
*Length: 16 inches*
*Width: 17 inches*
*Present owner: Newington Historical Society*
Mary Ann worked her Portsmouth sampler in silk on linen, enclosing the familiar scene along with verse, alphabets, and numerals as well as other decorative elements within an arcaded border interweaving leaf shapes. Alphabets and numerals occupy the upper portion of the sampler and are set off from the verse below by a narrow band of cross-stitch.

The verse "Firm on a rock with elevated mind/ Stands faith the conforter of human kind" is flanked by a pair of baskets that remain unfilled but were probably intended to hold mounded fruit.

A band of decorative cross-stitch separates the verse from the scene below, where one sees a house and barn with a birdhouse and a fence between them. Behind the fence are three trees but missing is the usual collection of birds. Below the scene she signed her work WROUGHT BY MISS MARY ANN DAVIS AGED 12 YEARS JULY 10TH 1828.

Mary Ann was probably the daughter of an E. Davis who operated a shop selling West Indies goods on Congress Street in Portsmouth.[141]

### Mary Ann Marden (1818–?)

*Sampler worked: 1828*
*Length: 16⅝ inches*
*Width: 16⅝ inches*
*Present owner: Jean Sawtelle*

Worked in silk on bleached linen and set within an arcarded border, Mary Ann included repetitions of the alphabet and numerals separated by simple bands of cross-stitch. Centering the sampler are lines of verse set within swagged and tasseled garlands and flanked by rounded baskets holding flowers.

The scene below includes a house at the left with a barn and birdhouse at the right and a fence separating the two buildings. Three trees stand behind the fence with birds perched in their branches. In typical fashion the sampler is signed at the base within an enclosed area that reads MISS MARY ANN MARDEN MARKED AT MFA HALL SCHOOL AGED 10.

She was probably the daughter of Jonathan and Sarah Marden. Jonathan was a joiner who lived on Ladd Street in Portsmouth.[142]

### Mary Elizabeth Drisco (1816–?)

*Sampler worked: 1828*
*Length: 16 inches*
*Width: 17 inches*
*Present owner: Stevens-Coolidge Place, North Andover, Massachusetts*

Working in silk on linen, Mary Elizabeth produced a Portsmouth sampler that bears all the hallmarks of its type. At the upper portion of the sampler she worked repetitions of the alphabet and numerals and then a centered verse within and extending to just below a pair of swagged garlands, all flanked by a pair of rounded baskets with flower blossoms, much like that worked by Mary Ann Davis.

At the lower portion Mary Elizabeth stitched the usual house and barn separated by a fence, behind which is a row of six trees with numerous birds perched among the branches. She personalized her rendering of the scene by adding other trees, one to the left of the house and one to the right of the barn. Her signature block appears below.

She was probably the daughter of the widow Mary Drisco, who was a communicant of St. John's Church in 1834, where Mary Elizabeth was baptized in 1836.[143]

**Frances Whidden** (1816–1855)
*Sampler worked: 1829*
*Length: 16½ inches*
*Width: 17½ inches*
*Present owner: Strawbery Banke Museum*
Working in silk on linen, Frances completed her memorial sampler, which she dedicated to her maternal grandparents, Anne and William Seavey. Anne died in 1826 and William in 1829.

Within a vine border Frances worked a unique sampler that includes repetitions of the alphabet and numerals. She centered a verse, "There is a calm for those who weep," flanked by an elderly man at left and woman at right inside a sawtooth frame along with her signature, FRANCES A. WHIDDEN AGED 13 YEARS HER/ UNDER THE TUITION OF E. ROBINSON PORTSMOUTH. The scene at the base of the sampler includes a graveyard at the center with a church building at left and a tree at right. Cherubs hover over the scene at either side of inscriptions commemorating the death dates of her grandparents.

She was the sister of Mary Ann Whidden, who was teaching needlework in Portsmouth in 1832, and Sarah L. Whidden, whose sampler is also discussed here and is preserved in the Newington Historical Society. Frances was the daughter of Joseph, a farmer, and Abby Whidden. She married Richard L. Palmer of Dorchester, Massachusetts.[144]

**Elizabeth Toscan Parrott** (1820–1841)
*Sampler worked: 1829*
*Dimensions: unknown*
*Present owner: Mrs. Merrill Spalding*

Elizabeth Toscan Parrott was the daughter of Enoch Greenleafe Parrott and Susannah Parker Parrott. Her mother was Susannah Parker, who worked a sampler in 1790.

The sampler is worked within an arcaded border with several repetitions of the alphabets in eyelet and cross-stitch. The inscription reads ELIZABETH TOSCAN PARROTT AGED 9 YEARS 1829, N.H. The base includes three small trees with a single bird on top of each one.

In a Remembrance Book to Elizabeth P. Spalding compiled in 1831–1838, Elizabeth Toscan Parrott wrote a poem to her teacher, Miss Spalding, in 1831.[145]

**Ann Pierce Drown** (dates unknown)
*Sampler worked: 1829*
*Length: 16½ inches*
*Width: 13 inches*
*Present owner: Portsmouth Historical Society*
Ann worked a very simple sampler in silk on linen that includes repetitions of the alphabet and numerals within an unadorned arcaded border. Perhaps the simplicity of her work was a reflection of the verse she chose to stitch. It reads, "Industry is the Path to Happiness." It would seem that she subscribed to the notion that brevity is the soul of wit and applied her industry elsewhere.

Ann was a daughter of Thomas P. and Mehitable Cutts Appleton Drown, who were married in 1806. She married Joseph W. Ham in Philadelphia in 1841. They had two children.[146]

**Maria Tufton Ladd** (1821–1835)
*Sampler worked: 1830*
*Length: 16 inches*
*Width: 12½ inches*
*Present owner: anonymous*
Five alphabets and two sets of numerals are stitched in silk on linen on this simply worked sampler that apparently was begun in December 1829. Maria also included a verse in her work and the couplet "The spark of piety and virtue, pursued with a firm and/ constant spirit, will assuredly lead to happiness."

Once finished with her needlework project, Maria was granted little time to practice the pursuit of piety or virtue. Within five years, at the young age of fourteen, she died. She was the ninth born of thirteen children, five of whom died before her. The following year, in 1836, her two last-born sisters, ages eight and five, also died.

Her parents were Alexander Ladd, son of Eliphalet Ladd of Exeter, and Maria Tufton Haven, who was the daughter of Nathaniel Haven and granddaughter of John Tufton Mason. Alexander Ladd's biographer described him as a man who "gave liberally of his time and means to all measures designed to raise the intellectual and moral tone, or to restore the declining business prosperity of Portsmouth, and for many other worthy purposes."

The family lived in a house on Pleasant Street that is today known as the Livermore House and has since been moved to Livermore Street.[147]

### Ruth Hall Nutter (1822–?)

*Sampler worked: circa 1830*
*Dimensions: unknown*
*Present owner: Strawbery Banke Museum*

Ruth worked four alphabets and a series of numerals in silk on linen and enclosed them within a vigorous arcaded border. In the lower portion of the sampler she signed her name, RUTH H. NUTTER'S SAMPLER BORN AUG. 17TH, 1822. At the base she worked an oblong container decorated with a diamond motif and filled it with exuberant floral forms. This she flanked with a pair of smaller containers of a similar form and decoration, along with a pair of beakers holding still more flowers.

Ruth was the sister of Nancy Ham Nutter, who worked a sampler at about the same time. They were the daughters of Ruth Hall and William Shackford Nutter, who had settled in Waterborough Centre, Maine.

Other examples of Ruth's needlework survive at Strawbery Banke in the form of a candlewicked coverlet. Dimity bedhangings that she is thought to have worked on are also preserved at the museum.

Ruth married Seth Philpot of Waterborough, Maine, on December 5, 1843. They had two children, William, born in 1844, and Susie, born in 1851.[148]

### Nancy Ham Nutter (1818–?)

*Sampler worked: circa 1830*

*Dimensions: unknown*
*Present owner: Strawbery Banke Museum*
Nancy worked four repetitions of the alphabet and a set of numerals in silk on linen ground. In the lower portion of her needlework she stitched a basket of flowers flanked by boughs of blossoms and signed the sampler NANCY H. NUTTERS SAMPLER BORN FEB. 17TH 1818. Like her sister Ruth, Nancy was either shy about revealing her age or they both decided to eliminate this information from their samplers at a later date.

Nancy Ham Nutter married William Augustus Kimball in October 1841, when he was still a law student. They made their home in Rochester, New Hampshire, where they became an influential family. They had two children. John William was born in 1844, and Lizzie Hale Kimball in 1851. Lizzie died six months short of her fourteenth birthday in 1865.[149]

## Mary Augusta Shapleigh (1818–?)
*Sampler worked: 1831*
*Length: $22\frac{1}{4}$ inches*
*Width: $12\frac{3}{4}$ inches*
*Present owner: Jean Sawtelle*
Mary worked bands of numerals and alphabets in silk on a green linsey-woolsey ground. She followed this with a band centering her name, MARY A. SHAPLEIGH AGED 13 AD 1831, which she flanked with inscriptions left and right:

> Our moments lie apace          Well if our days must
> Nor will our minutes            fly. We'll keep their
> stay. Just like a flood         end in sight., We'll sp
> our hasty days Are              end them all in wisdom
> sweeping us away                way. And let their Flight them speed.

The lower section of the sampler centers a vase with handles that contains stylized flowers upon which birds perch. The base is flanked by miniature trees and leaves as well as small birds. Above this are a pair of slope-sided baskets with rounded fruit and four small birds intertwined with large, tuliplike blooms.

Mary Augusta was the sixth of seven children born to Capt. Elisha Shapleigh and Martha Fernald Shapleigh of Eliot, Maine. He was a farmer. Mary Augusta married Dennis Ferguson of Eliot, Maine, on May 28, 1839.[150]

**Eliza Jane Wilson** (1819–?)
*Sampler worked: 1831*
*Dimensions: unknown*
*Present owner: unknown*
Worked in silk on unbleached linen are a pair of alphabets and a set of numerals. These appear above a family genealogical register with Eliza Jane's name and age centered within an arcade. What follows below is a typical Portsmouth scene depicting a two-story house with a fence, trees, barn, and birdhouse. Rather than sitting atop the fence, the birds in this scene are found perched on flowers arranged in an urn that she has placed at the right of the landscape scene.

The format is unusual and the design a tightly conceived and executed one, suggesting the hand and guidance of an experienced needleworker.

Eliza was the daughter of the Hon. Gowen and Nancy Fernald Wilson of Kittery, Maine. She married William Wentworth on October 22, 1843. They had three children: John Frederick, who died six days after his birth in 1845; Ann Eliza, born in 1847, who died at about fifteen; and Arville, who was born in 1849 and married John B. Trefethen in 1872. Trefethen was the adopted son of the Rev. Daniel Austin of Kittery.[151]

**Ann Mary Gerrish** (1821–1850)
*Sampler worked: 1832*
*Length: $17\frac{1}{4}$ inches*
*Width: $16\frac{1}{2}$ inches*
*Present owner: Betty Ring*
Ann used silk on linen to execute repetitions of the alphabet and numerals in almost perfect cadence. She also depicted a trio of two-story dwellings with fanlit central doors and fences standing before them. The buildings stand first in a pair just below the alphabets with lines of verse and a vertical banner of letters between them.

Below this scene she recorded her name, ANN M. GERRISH AGED 10 YEARS PORTSMOUTH AUGUST 20, 1832. The third building is centered here between baskets of mounded fruit and trees rendered in stylized diamond shapes. The whole is enclosed within a border of rings.

Ann was the daughter of Samuel and Mary Fernald Gerrish and married Thomas H. Odion, a mast and block maker.[152]

**Mary Ellen Cleaves** (1821–1863)
*Sampler worked: 1832*
*Dimensions: unknown*
*Present owner: Moffatt-Ladd House*
Mary Ellen chose a slightly abbreviated edition of the familiar Portsmouth landscape for her sampler worked in silk on linen. Along with repetitions of the alphabet and numerals, she depicted the customary house on a reduced scale and only a duo of trees behind the fence separating the barn and birdhouse from the house. Flanking this are a pair of neatly executed baskets of flowers, each with a vine trailing upward to balance the scene. At the base she stitched MARY ELLEN CLEAVES WROUGHT THIS IN 1832 JUNE. The whole is enclosed within an arcaded border.

She was the daughter of Deacon Samuel Cleaves. Mary Ellen married Horton Walker, a chandler who seems to have been her father's business partner. She died at the age of forty-two in 1863.[153]

**Caroline Elizabeth Currier** (1821–1883)
*Sampler worked: 1832*
*Length: 17 inches*
*Width: 12 inches*
*Present owner: Portsmouth Historical Society*
Working in silk on linen, Caroline laboriously completed six repetitions of the alphabet and a set of numerals. She followed them with the familiar verse "Jesus permit they gracious name."

The verse is decorated with the addition of flower-filled baskets, birds, and doglike animals at either side. The inscription WROUGHT BY CAROLINE E. CURRIER AUGUST 30, 1832 AGED 11 appears at the base.

Caroline was the daughter of Capt. Caleb and Sarah Marden Currier. She married John Stewart in 1849 and they had one daughter, Mary, born in 1857.[154]

**Sarah Elizabeth Marden** (1822–?)
*Sampler worked: 1832*
*Length: 21 inches*
*Width: 17 inches*
*Present owner: Jean Sawtelle*
Worked in silk on linen, Sarah's sampler includes four repetitions of the

alphabet and a row of numerals. The row of numerals is decorated with birds at either end. The verse "Jesus permit they gracious name ..." follows the alphabets and is flanked with containers of mounded fruit so familiar in other Portsmouth samplers.

The scene depicted at the bottom of the sampler includes a house and barn separated by a fence upon which birds perch. Birds are also to be found in a pair of trees near the house and a third tree near the barn. At the sampler's base is the inscription SARAH ELIZABETH MARDEN AE 10 HER WORK UNDER THE TUITION OF M. A. WHIDDEN PORTSMOUTH 1832. Flanking the inscription are flower-filled vases.

Sarah was the daughter of James Marden and Mercy Page Marden of Portsmouth, New Hampshire. On March 21, 1841, she married Daniel Brewster of Wolfeboro, New Hampshire.

Her teacher, Mary Ann Whidden, was the daughter of Joseph Whidden, a farmer living on Long Lane Road in Portsmouth, New Hampshire. On January 12, 1839, the *Portsmouth Journal* reported her death at the age of twenty-four.[155]


**Mary Jane Lear** (1820–1895)
*Sampler worked: 1833*
*Length: 21 inches*
*Width: 12 inches*
*Present owner: private collection*
Stitched on green linsey-woolsey, Mary Jane created a memorial for her two young brothers. Although she included three repetitions of the alphabet, it is clearly the decorative aspects that were to be the heart of this needlework. Mary Jane stitched SACRED IS THE MEMORY OF HIRAM LEAR WHO DEPARTED THIS LIFE SEPTEMBER 8, 1831 AGED 4 MONTHS and IN MEMORY OF NATHANIEL LEAR WHO DEPARTED THIS LIFE DECEMBER 7, 1832.

At the center and within a diamond-shaped lozenge is found, along with a pair of birds, the familiar Portsmouth scene composed of a house, a fence with a bird on it, a birdhouse, and a barn. The usual trees are missing in this rendition and are replaced by two large baskets of mounded fruit.

Mary was the daughter of Nathaniel (1792–1868) and Mary Lear (1795–1880) and was descended from Tobias Lear, secretary to George Washington.[156]

**Frances E. Litchfield** (1832–?)
*Sampler worked: 1833*
*Length: 16 inches*
*Width: 17 inches*
*Present owner: Strawbery Banke Museum*

Within a vigorous border of foliage and flowers, Frances worked a silk-on-linen sampler composed of familiar Portsmouth elements in a style that seems to have been hers alone.

Her repetitions of the alphabet into which the vined border charmingly encroaches end with the date June the 7, 1833. Just below, her signature line follows: FRANCES E. LITCHFIELD AGED 10 YRS. as the preface to a verse expressing the virtues of industry:

> When youth's soft seasons shall be over
> and [s]cenes of childhood charm no more
> My riper years with joy may se
> This youthful Proof of industry
> As memory oer this task shall wake
> And retrospective Pleasure take
> How shall I wish but wish in vain
> To enjoy youths careless hours again.

With the space remaining after her rather lengthy verse, she filled the base of the sampler with a house situated near a small grove of trees and at the right placed a large footed basket or urn filled with a strawberry plant bearing fruit.

She was probably the daughter of Joseph Litchfield, Esq., of Kittery, Maine, whose name appears in the Maine Census of 1820.

**Mary Elizabeth Wentworth** (1824–?)
*Sampler worked: 1835*
*Length: 15½ inches*
*Width: 17 inches*
*Present owner: Maine State Museum*

Worked in silk on unbleached linen, Mary Elizabeth's skillfully produced sampler reflects neatly planned symmetry. Cleanly worked alphabets that fit precisely within the sampler's border are followed by her signature, MARY ELIZABETH WENTWORTH AE 11 YEARS DEC 10 1835.

The lower half of her sampler is devoted to the rendering of the verse, "How blest the Maid whom circling Years improve ..." within a

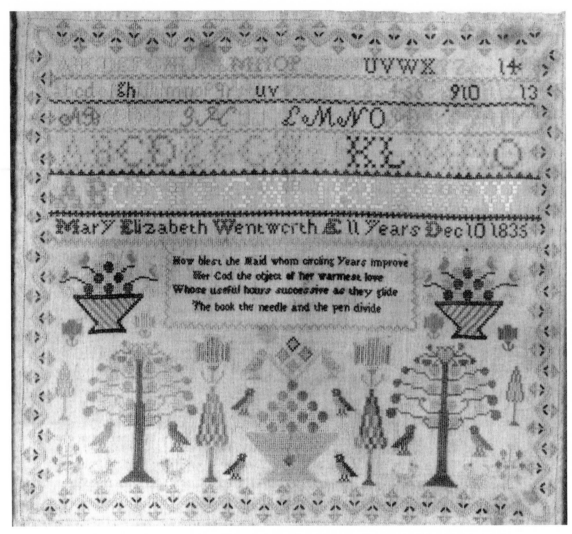

*Sampler worked by Mary Elizabeth Wentworth in 1835. Courtesy of the Maine State Museum. Greg Hart photograph.*

sawtooth bordered "tablet." This is surrounded by a variety of baskets mounded with fruit, and with birds, trees rendered in stepped geometric forms, and dogs. Many of these forms appear on other samplers worked in the Portsmouth and Piscataqua River region and the baskets can be seen in a sampler worked by Caroline Currier in 1832. The small dogs with their tails neatly curled and the birds seated in their steady pose also appear in the sampler worked by Sarah Jane Folsom in 1826.

Mary Elizabeth was the daughter of John and Betsey Fernald Wentworth of Kittery, Maine. She married the Rev. A. Perkins and had one son, John, born January 2, 1831.[157]

## Elizabeth Fabyan Willey (1821–?)
*Sampler worked: 1834*
*Length: 19 inches*
*Width: 17 inches*
*Present owner: Portsmouth Historical Society*
Within an arcaded border of rose blossoms, Elizabeth worked an ambitious silk-on-linen genealogical sampler. Neatly worked rows of repetitions of the alphabet and numerals occupy the upper portion of her sampler. At the center section a tasseled double garland encloses genealogical information about the Willey family. The swags are flanked by a pair of bulbous baskets with handles, filled with large, opened rose blossoms.

Below and at the center she placed a large basket with ornately scrolled handles. Within the basket is an array of floral blossoms. Standing at either side of the basket are trees rendered in bold geometric forms nearly identical to those found in the sampler worked by Ann M. Gerrish in 1832. Also included within this placement of basket and trees are birds, both placed upon the ground and perched on smaller renderings of the geometric trees. She signed her work ELIZABETH FABYAN WILLEY HER SAMPLER AGED 12 WROUGHT DECEMBER 1834 * GOD IS LOVE.

Elizabeth was the daughter of Stephen and Elizabeth Hoit Willey. In 1839 she married William Innis in Portsmouth.[158]

## Mary Frances Folsom (1824–1912)
*Sampler worked: 1835*
*Length: 15 inches*
*Width: 15½ inches*

*Present owner: Portsmouth Historical Society*
Mary Frances, the only needlework student we found to have seen the dawn of the twentieth century, produced a pleasing silk-on-linen sampler. The simple format of alphabets, verse, and small flower- and fruit-filled baskets is contained within an unadorned arcaded border punctuated by alternating starlike flower shapes. The verse

> Virtue is the chiefest beauty of the mind
> The noblest ornament of the human kind
> Remember death think every day the last
> Lament all vanities and follies Past

is followed by Mary's signature enclosed within a tablet shape formed of simple cross-stitch. It reads MARY F. FOLSOM/ AGED 11 YRS/ JULY 15 1835 and at either side the tablet is flanked by baskets.

She was the daughter of Nathaniel and Mary Smith Folsom and the twin sister of James William Folsom. On July 15, 1845, she married Nathan F. Mathes. They had two daughters, Frances and Ellen. A sampler worked by her sister, Sarah, in 1826 is also included in this survey.[159]


**Martha Jane Fowler** (1821–?)
*Sampler worked: 1835*
*Length: 21 inches*
*Width: 17¼ inches*
*Present owner: Kent B. Willis*
Within an arcaded border punctuated with maple leaves, Martha worked her silk-on-linen sampler in the Portsmouth tradition established some dozen years earlier. Here, crowded together in neat profusion, are all of the elements one expects to find in such a needlework.

Alphabets and numerals mark the upper portion of the sampler, followed by a rendering of the following verse:

> May guardian angels their kind wings display
> And guide you safe through every distant way
> To every place may you most happy be
> And though far distant often think on me
> Virtue the strength and beauty of the soul
> Is the best gift of Heaven.

Standing at either side of the verse are small baskets holding viny sprays of foliage. Below, a pair of angels, like those found in at least eight other samplers, hold a banner outstretched above a now familiar landscape. At the far left a basket with sloping sides is filled with blossoms. Across the remainder of the landscape one finds a brick house with shuttered windows, some open and some closed. A fence joins the house to a barn or carriage house and encloses trees worked in two different forms, a birdhouse atop a pole, and an array of birds.

Her signature occupies two lines at the base of the sampler, MARTHA JANE FOWLER WORKED THIS IN THE 14 YEAR OF HER AGE BORN MARCH 22ND/ 1822 OCTOBER 21 1835 PORTSMOUTH, N. H. She was the daughter of the joiner Paul Fowler and Phebe Reding Fowler. After 1839 Paul Fowler no longer appears in the Portsmouth City Directory and so the family may have moved to another town sometime between 1835 and 1839.[160]

**Margaret Jane Ball** (1825–?)
*Sampler worked: 1837*
*Length: 17 inches*
*Width: 16½ inches*
*Present owner: Strawbery Banke Museum*
Margaret worked her sampler in silk on linen. Several repetitions of the alphabet and numerals are neatly laid out in the upper portion of her sampler. Below she stitched the well-known verse "Jesus permit Thy gracious name ..." and placed small baskets mounded with fruit in a pyramid fashion at either side. At the base of the sampler a pair of larger baskets, one containing strawberry plants and the other flowers, flank her signature, WROUGHT BY/ MARGARET JANE BALL/ AE 12 YEARS/ 1837. A scrolled border incorporating flower blossoms encloses the entire sampler.

**Sarah E. Gerrish** (1827–?)
*Sampler worked: 1839*
*Dimensions: unknown*
*Present owner: anonymous*
Sarah, about whom very little is known, worked a charmingly naïve version of the Portsmouth motif in silk on coarse linen. She was

twelve when she set needle to fabric and produced a sampler that appears to have represented a laborious task for her. Within a simple border of alternating colors she set down three repetitions of the alphabet and one set of numerals followed by this verse:

> The canvas thus in colors laid
> Gives a just emblem of mankind
> Thus education good or bad
> Shows on the canvas of the mind.

Fruit piled pyramid fashion in slope-sided baskets can be seen at either side of the verse. A crossband of scrolling cross-stitch separates the verse from her signature line, WROUGHT BY SARAH E. GERRISH AGED 12 YEARS 1839.

At the base of the sampler appears a simple house with two shuttered windows, one open and the other closed. A fence behind which stand two trees joins the house to a barn. At the barnyard gate, a large bird sits upon the gatepost.

The *Journal* of January 1, 1853, reports that Miss Sarah E. Gerrish was married to Mr. Andrew J. Whidden.[161]

**Sarah Emily Currier** (1824–1893)
*Sampler worked: 1840*
*Length: 23¾ inches*
*Width: 23½ inches*
*Present owner: Portsmouth Historical Society*

As though on cue, Sarah Emily Currier worked a sampler in 1840 that would become a tribute to the expression of the needle arts in Portsmouth in the eighteenth and nineteenth centuries. She very skillfully rendered a work of enormous proportions that incorporates all of the finest elements of all those that came before hers.

Within a complex border of sawtooth and berry motifs, she executed cleanly struck repetitions of the alphabet and numerals decorated with a pair of slope-sided baskets holding sprays of berry blossoms. Below the alphabets are a pair of finely worked garlands of flowers suspended by bowed ribbons. These flank a smaller tasseled garland held aloft by a pair of angels. Within this garland appear her initials, SEC.

Occupying the lower section of the sampler is the familiar Portsmouth landscape, this time set around a large basket filled with elaborately worked flowers in a variety of forms. At left is a brick house with a fence, tree, and birdhouse on a pole, and at the right is a brick barn with a fence and trees.

A modest signature line appears below the scene, WROUGHT BY SARAH EMILY CURRIER JUNE 20 1840 AGED 16. The oldest of the students whose work we have seen, Sarah was the daughter of Captain Caleb and Sarah Marden Currier and was one of five children.[162]

Sarah E. Currier married John J. Marston in 1849.

# *Appendix*

Sarah P. Horney was the daughter of Capt. Gilbert and Theodora Horney. The guardianship expense account reproduced on the following pages was filed by William Simes on behalf of Sarah for the years 1806 to 1815. The original is in the Rockingham County, New Hampshire, Probate Office. The guardianship expired in 1815 and the next year Sarah became a teacher of needlework. She died unmarried in 1834.

William Simes      Account of his Guardia

| | | | |
|---|---|---:|---:|
| | The said Guardian charges the following Sums | | |
| | Some third expences on the Estate from | | |
| | June 18th 1806 to May 29th 1807 | 52 | 99 |
| | one Quarter the expences on the Estate | | |
| 1806 | from May 29th 1807 to Aug.t 21st 1809 | 154 | 10 |
| July 19 | Cash p.d Mrs Hart for her Schooling | 6 | 15 |
| | paid for Books & quills | " | 37½ |
| Oct.r 17 | paid Mrs Hart for her Schooling | 5 | 53 |
| Dec.r 31 | Cash p.d Mr & J. Horney for Boarding & | | |
| | Cloathing from March 4th to Dec.r 31st | 66 | 89 |
| | Cash p.d Mr & J. Horney for Boarding | | |
| 1807 | & Cloathing from Jan.y 1st to May 29th 1807 | 33 | 12 |
| Jan.r 15 | 1 Writing Book | " | 12½ |
| May 27 | 1 Small Book | " | 12½ |
| July 6 | Quill & Books | " | 37½ |
| 13 | Cash p.d Mr Hart for Schooling | 5 | 43 |
| Aug.t 4 | 1 Burel Quill & 3 Books | " | 62½ |
| Nov.r 12 | Cash p.d Mrs Hart for Schooling | 5 | 55 |
| | Cash p.d for Boarding & Cloathing | | |
| 1808 | from May 29-1807 to May 28-1808 | 80 | 11 |
| June 15 | To 1 Trunk containing wearing Apparell | 60 | " |
| | 1 pair Silver Sugar Tongs | 3 | " |
| | 1 Gold Pin | 2 | 75 |
| | 1 Trunk | 3 | 75 |
| July 14 | one quarter the Jewells as p.r S. Barking bill | " | 87½ |
| | Cash p.d for Articles for Mourning p.r bill | 19 | 27 |
| | Sundry expences for dancing School | 4 | 62½ |
| 21 | Cash to buy Cambric 1/10½ Ribbon 1/3 | | |
| | Paint Box 1/6/6 | 3 | 26½ |
| | Cash p.d J Hart for Schooling p.r bill | 6 | 80 |
| | Cash p.d George Dame for Schooling | 6 | 83 |
| Oct.r | 1 Thimble 4½ Cash 2/ | " | 40 |
| 16 | half of B. Brierley's bill | 10 | 46 |
| | D.o N. B. Moulton's Bill | 2 | 57½ |
| | Cash p.d John Welcher for Buttons | " | 62½ |

| | | |
|---:|---:|
| | 319 | 15½ |
| | 158 | 9 |
| | 59 | 47 |
| Amount carried Up | 536 | 72 |

...nship for Sarah P Horney

| | | | |
|---|---|---|---|
| 1807 | The said Guardian credits the following sums | | |
| May 29 | By one third of the Rent of the Estate from June 18th 1806 to May 29th 1807 — together with the balance remaining in my hands June 18 1806 | 78 | 87 | |
| | By one quarter the rents of the Estate from May 29th 1807 – to Augt 21 – 1809 } | 126 | 68 | |
| | One quarter the Nt proceeds of personal Estate | 170 | 84 | |
| | By amot of Andrew Halliburton's present to her | 83 | 75 | |
| | „ one quarter Sales of the Real Estate - - - | 875 | ~ | 1335 „ 14 |
| | | | | |
| 1808 | To Amount of Debt Brought Up | | | 536 „ 7½ |
| Octr 16 | „ Cash to buy Stockings - - - - - - | 1 | ~ | |
| | „ Cash pd her Octr 24th - - - - - - | „ | 62 | |
| Decr 8 | „ Cash to buy Silk - - - - - - - | „ | 10 | |
| | „ Cash pd for dying Gown - - - - | 2 | „ | |
| | „ Cash to buy Silk - - - - - - | „ | 50 | |
| | „ Cash pd Saml Mudge for Shoes - | 4 | 59 | 8 „ 81½ |
| 1809 | „ Cash pd S Hart for Schooling - - - | 8 | 93 | |
| | „ Cash 3/- 1 pair Knitting Pins 6d | „ | 56 | |
| | „ Mending Umbrella - - - - - | „ | 75 | |
| Mar 19 | „ Cash 1/6 - Cash to buy Cotton - - 6d | 1 | 25 | |
| apl 16 | „ 1 Book & Bunch Quills - - - - - 1/6 | „ | 37½ | |
| | „ Cash to buy Vandyke 4/6 - do to buy Cotton 2d | „ | 95 | |
| May 10 | „ Cash - - - - - - - - - | „ | 10 | |
| | „ Cash to Mrs Halliburton for fifty two week board from June 6 1808 to June 6 1809 } at 7/6 per Week - - - - | 65 | „ | |
| | Cash pd Mrs Halliburton for fifteen week board at 7/6 per week - - } | 18 | 75 | 96 „ 66½ |
| June 12 | To Cash 3/- 20th Cash 2/7½ - - - - | „ | 94 | |
| 27 | „ Cash pd L Draper - - - - - - | 3 | 75 | |
| | „ Do pd Mr Odione - - - - - | „ | 42 | |
| | „ Cash to buy Cotton - - - - - | „ | 25 | |
| | „ one third of Dr Humphries bill | 8 | 03 | |
| | „ Cash 3/- Cash 2/- - - - | „ | 84 | 14 „ 23 |
| | Amount Carried Over | | | 656 „ 4½ |

| | | | | |
|---|---|---|---|---|
| | Amount Brought Forward | | | 656„43 |
| 1809 | S. B. Griffith, note for one quarter the rent of Store | 13 | „ | |
| Sep.t 9 | To Cash p.d for tapping Shoes | „ | 58 | |
| | „ Cash 3/- Cash p.d J. Hart for Schooling 9.17½ | 9 | 67½ | |
| Oct.r 11 | „ Cash 1/3, Cash 13.d | „ | 32 | 1815 |
| | „ Cash p.d J. Hart for Schooling | 7 | 50 | Sept. |
| 20 | „ Cash for Sundries from O. B.ward | 5 | 75 | |
| | „ do for Sundries | „ | 69½ | |
| Nov. 27 | „ Cash for cotton 9/- Cash 4/6- Cash 6/- | 1 | 87½ | |
| Dec.r 4 | „ Cash | „ | 56 | 39„95½ |
| 15 | To Sundries 70.d 1 Skein Yarn | „ | 80 | |
| | „ Board from Sept.r 22 to Dec.r 27 at 7/6 week | 17 | 17 | |
| 1810 | „ Cash p.d R. Mendum, Bill | 1 | 33 | |
| Feby 12 | „ Cash 12/- 15- Cash 6/- 21- Cash 18/9 | 6 | 12½ | |
| Mar. 24 | „ Cash 1/6- May 21- Cash 24/- | 4 | 25 | |
| | „ Cash p.d Miss Purcells Bill | 85 | „ | |
| June 12 | „ Cash 12/- Aug.t 8- Cash 12/- | 4 | „ | |
| Aug.t 14 | „ 1 p.r Shoe 8/- Cash do Ann 6/- | 2 | 34 | |
| | „ p.d W.m Jones per Bill | 1 | „ | |
| | „ p.d Sam.l Mudge per Bill | 4 | 92 | |
| Sept.r 1 | 1 Comb 6/- 11- Cash 6/- do 12/- do 12/- do 30/- | 10 | 50 | 137„43½ |
| | „ Cash p.d W.m Jones bill | 2 | 92 | |
| Nov. 28 | Cash 6/- Dec.r 14- Cash 6/- | 2 | 00 | |
| Dec.r 14 | Cash p.d Miss Purcell | 35 | 40 | |
| Mar. 7 1811 | To Cash 6/- Cash 9/- | 2 | 50 | |
| 25 | „ Balance due on Gold wires | „ | 75 | |
| | „ Cash 24/- May 7- Cash 12/- 15.th Cash 18/- | 9 | „ | |
| June 10 | „ Mending Thimble | „ | 20 | |
| July 2 | „ Cash 6/- 20.th 1 p.r Scissors 1/6 | 1 | 25 | |
| Feby 3 1812 | „ Cash 12/ Feby 6.th Cash 18/- 25- 12/- | 9 | „ | |
| Mar. 23 | „ Cash 18/- May 22- do 30/- do 42/- | 15 | „ | 78„32 |
| June 14 1813 | „ Cash $12 Aug.t 27.th Cash $6 | 18 | „ | |
| Sept.r 24 | „ Cash $6- Nov.r 2- Cash $12 | 18 | „ | |
| | to one third loss on Mortgage Sold S. Sheafe | 33 | 33½ | |
| 1814 | 1/3 of 15/ p.d C. R. Freeman Esq.r | „ | 83½ | |
| Mar. 3 | „ Cash 36/- Aug.t 17- Cash $13 | 19 | „ | |
| Mar. 6 1816 | „ Cash $15- Cash p.d for wood &c 11/3 | 16 | 87½ | |
| Apr.l 10 | „ Cash nine dollars | 9 | „ | 115„04 |
| | | | | 1027„18 |

William Times

Amount of Debt brot forward — $104.18

" " Horse & Chain

" 30 " had probate fees —

                                          B
                                    $3033 = 15
Balance due the ward —         301. 96
                              $1 335 . 14

By amount of Credit to the Ward £1335.14

I consent to the allowance of this account

                    Sarah P. Hooway.

Rockingham ss Probate Court Exeter Sep 30.1815

This account was exhibited for
allowance sworn to by the Ac-
-countant & consented to by the
ward — is allowed —

                    Nath Rogers

Acct of Nath Gimes the
Guard of Sarah P. Hooway
Sep 30, 1815.

# Notes

1.  John Cosens Ogden, *The Female Guide or Thoughts on That Education of the Sex Accommodated to the State of Society, Manners and Government, in the United States,* St. John's Church, Portsmouth, N.H. (Concord, N.H.: Hough, 1793), p. 50.

2.  *Ibid.*

3.  *New Hampshire Gazette and General Advertiser*, May 5, 1790.

4.  Dr. Benjamin Rush, *Thoughts Upon Females Education, Accommodated to the Present State of Society, Manners, and Government in the U.S.A.* (Philadelphia, 1787).

5.  U. S. Census 1750.

6.  On January 1, 1801, the Rev. Timothy Alden delivered "The Glory of America, a Century Sermon" in which he talks of the bright future awaiting Portsmouth and describes what he saw as the signs of prosperity here.

7.  Ogden, *The Female Guide*, p. 5.

8.  Charles Burroughs, "An Address on Female Education" delivered in Portsmouth, New Hampshire, October 26, 1827 (Childs and March publishers).

9.  Rev. Timothy Alden, "The Glory of America, a Century Sermon" (Portsmouth, 1801). The "mechanic" referred to by Alden in this passage is the artisan/craftsman in general.

10. Ethel Stanwood Bolton and Eva Johnston Coe, *American Samplers* (Boston, 1921), p. 267. Identified as verse number 94.

11. Alden, "The Glory of America, a Century Sermon."

12.     John P. Peters, *Diary of David McClure, Doctor of Divinity 1748–1820* (New York, 1899), pp. 148–149.

13.     Rockingham County, New Hampshire Register of Probate. James Kenney, 1822. #0000.

14.     *New Hampshire Gazette*, March 12, 1780.

15.     *New Hampshire Gazette,* April 30, 1791.

16.     *New Hampshire Gazette*, September 26, 1791.

17.     Nathaniel Dearborn, *Boston Notions* (Boston: Printed by Nathaniel Dearborn).

18.     Rockingham County, New Hampshire, Probate Office. Will dated August 16, 1821.

19.     *New Hampshire Gazette*, March 31, 1801.

20.     Certificate issued to Master John Greenleaf at the Reverend Mr. Alden's Academy at Portsmouth, N.H., Demarara Street, October 13, 1806. In the collections of the New York Historical Society, New York, New York.

21.     Catherine Whipple Langdon, *Journal of Catherine Whipple Langdon* (1803). Warner House Association archives at Portsmouth Athenaeum.

22.     From the South Parish (Portsmouth, N.H.) Record Book #4, 1749 to 1833. Entry for April 23, 1805.

23.     *Ibid*. Entry for June 10, 1805.

24.     Joseph Foster, *Colonel Joseph Foster, His Children and Grandchildren* (Hartford, Conn., 1935), pp. 179–183.

25.     List of Young Ladies who attended the Misses Martin's School. Maine Historical Society, Portland, Maine, 1804 to 1829.

26.     *Portsmouth City Directory* 1827.

27.     *Portsmouth Gazette*, Oct. 27, 1818, "Miss Walden's Drawing School will be continued throughout the Winter—three mornings in a week, at her Father's House in Penhallow Street."

28.     *New Hampshire Gazette*, March 29 and April 19, 1808.

29.     From the Journal of Sarah Parker Rice Goodwin in the collections of Strawbery Banke Museum, Portsmouth, New Hampshire.

30.     "Parnassian Spring," *New Hampshire Gazette and General Advertiser,* May 5, 1790.

31.     Recorded in "A Charity Sermon" delivered by the Rev. Mr. Timothy Alden at the Portsmouth Female Asylum on September 1, 1804.

32.  Receipt in the archives of Strawbery Banke dated April 19, 1809. Mrs. Mary Chase to Lydia Peirce, "To schooling Miss Mary Toppan, one month [and] to schooling Miss Harrio(e)t Crosby, seven weeks. Rec'd payment [signed] Lydia Peirce."

33.  Recorded in the account books of the South Parish Church, Portsmouth, N.H.

34.  Rockingham County Probate Records, Exeter, N.H., dated September 30, 1815. Account of William Simes Guardianship of Sarah P. Horney.

35.  *New Hampshire Gazette*, March 10, 1812.

36.  Albert H. Hoyt, *Daniel Peirce of Newbury, Mass. 1638–1677* (Boston, 1875, privately printed).

37.  Rev. Thomas Davies, F.D.D., *Memoirs of Joshua Winslow Peirce* (Boston: reprinted with additions from the Historical and Genealogical Register, October 1874), printed for private distribution.

     David Parsons Holton ... and his wife, Mrs. Frances K. Winslow Holton, *Memorial. Family Records of The Winslows and Their Descendants in America, with The English Ancestry as Far as Known* (New York: D.P. Holton, 1877–88), Vol. II, 1888.

     Maria Whitman Bryant, *Genealogy of Edward Winslow of the Mayflower and his Descendants from 1620–1865* (Pembroke, Mass., 1915).

38.  Edited by Alice Morse Earle, *Diary of Anna Green Winslow—A Boston School Girl of 1771* (New York: Houghton, Mifflin and Co., and Cambridge: The Riverside Press, 1894).

39.  Pearce W. Penhallow, Esq. of Boston, *Memoirs of the Penhallow Family*, New Hampshire Historical Genealogical Records, Vol. 32, 1878.

40.  John Wentworth, *The Wentworth Genealogy: English and American. Vol. I* (Boston: Little Brown & Co., 1878), pp. 329–331.

41.  Sybil Noyes et al., *General Dictionary of Maine and New Hampshire*. Baltimore, Ohio: Genealogical Publishing Co., 1972), p. 459.

42.  Gerald D. Foss, *Captain Hopley Yeaton Memorial* (St. John's Lodge No. 1, May, 1975).

43.  Elizabeth Knowles Folsom, *Genealogy of the Folsom Family 1638–1938. Vol I* (Rutland, Vt.: The Tuttle Publishing Co., 1938), pp. 190–191.

44.  Bolton and Coe, *American Samplers*, p. 40.

45.  D. Clapp & Son, *A History of the Cutter Family of New England. The Compilation of the late Dr. Benjamin Cutter et al.* (Boston, 1871).

46.  Index of Marriage Records of Rye, N.H. 1726–1899, p. 116.

47. Caroline Cole Hollingsworth, "Embroidery in the Society's Collection," *Old Time New England*, 1966, p. 69. The date given to the sampler in the article is incorrect and indicates that it was made in the 1750s.

48. Bolton and Coe, *American Samplers*, p. 74.

49. Wentworth, *The Wentworth Genealogy: English and American, Vol. I*, pp. 315–317.

50. J. M. Hart, *Hart Genealogy* (Concord State Library, Concord, New Hampshire).

51. Records of the South Church, Portsmouth, p. 299.

52. *Foster Genealogy,* pp. 245 & 268.

53. North Cemetery, Portsmouth, N.H. Tomb with marble plaque in memory of Submit Sherburne d. 1807, a. 28. Full text from New Hampshire Historical Society anonymous manuscript dated 1884.

54. Wentworth, *Wentworth Genealog,. Vol. 1*, pp. 329–331.

55. Bolton and Coe, *American Samplers*, p. 67.

56. Wentworth, *The Wentworth Genealogy, Vol. 1,* p. 310.

57. Receipt. Thayer Cumings Historical Reference Library, Strawbery Banke Museum, #76.1.52.

58. *Portsmouth Journal*, August 17, 1844.

59. *Records of the North Church, Portsmouth. N.H. 1779–1835*. Compiled by Mrs. Louise H. Rainey.

60. John Whiteman, *U.S. Trailblazer in Far East Saluted*, by Portsmouth Group *Portsmouth Herald*, Oct. 26, 1986.

61. Bolton and Coe, *American Samplers,* p. 72.

62. William Richard Cutter, *History of the Cutter Family of New England* (Boston, 1871), p.166.

63. Bolton and Coe, *American Samplers,* p. 86.

64. *Foster Genealogy,* pp.267–68.

65. Records of the South Church, Portsmouth, section 231.

66. *Portsmouth Directory,* 1821.

67. Ida May Robinson, *Items of Ancestry By a Descendant* (Boston: David Clapp & Son, 1894), pp. 28–29.

68. *New Hampshire Gazette*, April 11, 1766, and April 23, 1773.

69. Records of the South Church, Portsmouth, N.H., pp. 40, 289, 412.

70. Charles W. Brewster, *Rambles About Portsmouth* (Portsmouth: Lewis W. Brewster, 1869), Second Series, pp. 226, 297.

71. *New Hampshire Gazette,* December 27, 1808, February 15, 1825, and November 22, 1825.

72. Records of the South Church, Portsmouth. N.H., pp. 25, 422.

73. Records of the North Church, Portsmouth, N.H., Records of Baptisms, p. 475.

74. Records of the South Church, Portsmouth, N.H., p. 49.

75. *New Hampshire Gazette,* October 19, 1824.

76. Rev. Timothy Alden, *Catalogue of Pupils for the Quarter Ending XIII October MDCCC VII* (The Alden Academy, Portsmouth, N.H.).

77. *Ibid.*

78. C. E. Parsons, *History of Rye, N.H.* (unpublished manuscript), p. 569.

79. "The Rev. Mr. Alden's Academy, at Portsmouth, For The Instruction of Masters and Misses in Various Branches of Useful Knowledge" roster of pupils for 1803, 1806, 1807.

80. Records of the South Church of Portsmouth, N.H., p. 24.

81. Cecil Hampden Cutts Howard, *Genealogy of the Cutts Family in America* (Albany, N.Y.: Joel Munsell's Sons, 1892).

82. Bolton and Coe, *American Samplers,* p. 356, plate XCVIII.

83. James Creighton, *The Odiorne Family* (Boston: Rand, Avery & Co., 1875), p. 104.

84. Agnes Austin Aubin, *A Warner House Biography* (Boston: Benson, Vaughan & Johnstone, 1935, reprinted 1977), pp. 6–7.

85. C. W. Tarlton, *The Tarlton Family* (Concord, N.H.: I. C. Evans, 1906).

86. George Thomas Little, *The Little Genealogy* (Auburn, Maine, 1882), p. 284.

87. Bolton and Coe, *American Samplers,* p. 201.

88. Frank Albert Davis, "Christopher Noble and Some of His Descendants," *New England Historical & Genealogical Register,* vol. 94/95 (January 1941): 36–37.

89. William M. Emery, *The Salters of Portsmouth* (New Bedford, Mass. 1936), p. 40–42.

90. Bolton and Coe, *American Samplers,* p. 205.

91. Howard, *Genealogy of the Cutts Family in America,* p. 49.

92. Laura Fecych Sprague, editor, *Agreeable Situations* (Boston: Northeastern University Press, 1987), pp. 244–245.

93. Wentworth, *Wentworth Genealogy, Vol. II,* p. 313.

94. Howard, *Genealogy of the Cutts Family in America.*

95.     *Foster Genealogy,* pp. 244–46.

96.     John E. Frost, *Portsmouth Cemetery Records Vol II.*

97.     Bolton and Coe, *American Samplers,* p. 157.

98.     Records of the North Church, Portsmouth, N.H., pp. 5, 29.

99.     *New Hampshire Gazette,* November 19, 1842.

100.    New Hampshire Historical Society, *Decorative Arts of New Hampshire* (1973), fig. III, no. 143, pp. 60–61.

101.    Records of the South Church of Portsmouth, N.H.

102.    Charles H. Bell, *History of the Town of Exeter* (Exeter, N.H., 1888), p. 10.

103.    *Portsmouth Journal,* October 28, 1837.

104.    Records of the Central Baptist Church, Portsmouth. In the Portsmouth Athenaeum.

105.    *New Hampshire Gazette,* November 28, 1826.

106.    William M. Emery, *The Salters of Portsmouth* (New Bedford, Mass., 1936), p. 35.

107.    John E. Frost, *Portsmouth Record Book II,* pp. 15, 34.

108.    Records of the North Church, Portsmouth N.H., in the Ministry of Rev. Joseph Buckminster and Rev. Israel W. Putnam 1779–1835. Compiled by Mrs. Louise H. Rainey.

109.    Records of the South Church, Portsmouth, p. 28.

110.    *Portsmouth Journal,* July 6, 1849

111.    John Cogswell Badger, *Giles Badger and His Descendants* (Manchester, N.H.: John B. Clarke Co., 1909), p. 41.

112.    Perley M. Leighton, *New Hampshire Geneological Society Vol. I* (Boston, Mass., 1989), pp. 72–73.

113.    Ida May Robinson, *Items of Ancestry By a Descendant* (Boston: David Clapp & Son, 1894), pp. 28–29.

114.    James Creighton, *The Odiorne Family.* (Boston, Mass.: Rand, Avery and Co., 1875), p. 51.

115.    Frost, *Records of the North Cemetery Vol. I,* section 305.

116.    *Portsmouth Journal*, August 29, 1835.

117.    *Portsmouth City Directory* 1834.

118.    Catalogue & Synopsis of the First Female School in Portsmouth, N.H., March 1, 1827. Historical Society. MS22 at Portsmouth Athenaeum, Portsmouth, N.H.

119.    Records of the North Church of Portsmouth, N.H.

120. John E. Frost, *Portsmouth Record Book—Records of the South Cemetery Vol. II* (University Heights, N.Y., Feb. 25, 1955).

Records of the South Church of Portsmouth, N.H., pp. 25, 420.

*Portsmouth Journal,* November 1, 1834.

122. John E. Frost, *Portsmouth Record Book Vol. II* (New York, 1955), p. 140.

Wentworth, *Wentworth Genealogy Vol. II,* p. 63.

123. *Portsmouth Journal,* June 20, 1835.

Catalog of the First Female School of Portsmouth 1827.

Frost, *Records of North Centery Vol. I,* p 9.

124. *Portsmouth City Directory 1821,* p. 40.

125. *Portsmouth City Directory 1821* and *1827.*

*Portsmouth Gazette,* January 29, 1839.

Glee Krueger, *New England Samplers to 1840* (Old Sturbridge Village, 1978), pp. 36–37, 195.

126. *Portsmouth City Directory 1821* and *1827.*

*Portsmouth Journal & Rockingham Gazette,* August 15, 1829.

*Portsmouth Journal,* July 28, 1832.

Frost, *Portsmouth Record Book Vol. II,* p. 27.

127. Arthur C. Wiggin et al., *Wiggin Genealogy* (Concord, N.H: New Hampshire Historical Society).

*Portsmouth City Directory 1834.*

Leonard A. Morrison, *The History of the Sinclair Family in Europe and America* (Boston: Damrell & Upham, 1896).

128. *Portsmouth Directory 1827, 1834.*

*Portsmouth Journal,* May 14, 1842.

129. Langdon B. Parsons, *History of the Town of Rye* (Concord, N.H.: Rumford Printing Co., 1905), p. 294.

*Portsmouth City Directory 1839.*

130. Catalogue and Synopsis of the First Female School in Portsmouth, N.H., March 1, 1827.

*Portsmouth City Directory 1827.*

*Portsmouth Journal,* December 26, 1835.

131. *Portsmouth Journal,* December 16, 1837.

Frost, *Portsmouth Record Book Vol. II,* section 173.

132. Dori Faith Chadbourne, unpublished genealogical manuscript (Bethel, Maine, 1984).

133. Betty Ring, *American Needlework Treasures* (N.Y.: E.P. Dutton, 1987), p. 20.

   Will of Charles Reding, Rockingham (N.H.) County Probate Records #13664, January 1839.

134. *Portsmouth Journal*, September 5, 1840.

135. Frost, *Portsmouth Record Book Vol. II*, p. 9. Cemetery Inscription.

   *Portsmouth Journal,* March 28, 1840.

136. Ring, *American Needlework Treasures,* p. 21.

137. Records of South Church, Portsmouth, N.H., p. 186.

138. Elizabeth Knowles Folsom, *Genealogy of the Folsom Family 1638–1938 Vol. I* (Rutland, Vt.: Tuttle Publishing Co., 1938), pp. 199–200.

   *Portsmouth Journal*, March 19, 1836.

139. *Portsmouth Journal,* May 27, 1836.

   *Portsmouth City Directory 1827.*

   *New Hampshire Gazette*, October 3, 1825, and December 5, 1826.

   *Portsmouth City Directory 1827.*

   Frost, *Portsmouth Record Book Vol. II,* p. 27.

140. *Portsmouth City Directory 1827* and *1834.*

   New Hampshire Census 1840.

141. *Portsmouth City Directory 1827.*

142. *Portsmouth City Directory 1827* and *1839–40.*

   Sylvia Fitts Getchel, *Marden Family Genealogy* (privately printed, 1974).

143. Records of St. John's Church, Vol. I, 1795–1884, pp. 54, 61, 309.

144. Louise Tallman, *Portsmouth Families* (unpublished manuscript in the Portsmouth Athenaeum).

   *Portsmouth City Directory 1821, 1827,* and *1834.*

145. *Remembrance Book to Elizabeth P. Spalding 1831–1838,* Portsmouth Athenaeum Special Collections S-215.

146. Howard, *Genealogy of the Cutts Family in America,* pp. 55, 226.

   *Portsmouth Journal,* September 11, 1841.

147. Warren Ladd, *The Ladd Family, a Genealogical and Biographical Memoir of the Descendants of Ladd* (Bedford, Mass.: Edmund Anthony & Sons, 1890).

Howard, *Genealogy of the Cutts Family in America*, p. 218.

Frost, *Portsmouth Record Book Vol. II,* p. 6.

148. Wentworth, *The Wentworth Genealogy: English and American*, Vol. I: 482–484, Vol. II:62.

149. *Ibid.*

150. Hannah C. S. Tibbetts and Frederick E. Shapleigh, *Shapleigh Family Genealogy* (Kennebunkport, Me.: Star Press, 1968).

151. Wentworth, *The Wentworth Genealogy: English and American*, Vol. II: 746.

Everett S. Stackpole, *Old Kittery and Her Families* (Lewiston, Maine: Lewiston Journal Co., 1903), p. 802.

152. Howard, *Genealogy of the Cutts Family in America,* p. 102

153. Frost, *Portsmouth Record Book Vol. I,* p. 113.

*Portsmouth City Directory 1834* and *1839–40.*

154. Currier Family Bible in the Portsmouth Historical Society.

Frost, *Portsmouth Record Book Vol. I,* p. 164.

155. Sylvia Fitts Getchell, *Marden Family Genealogy, 1974.*

C. C. Lord, *A History of the Descendants of Nathan Lord of Ancient Kittery, ME* (Concord, N.H.: The Rumford Press, 1912), p. 11.

Langdon B. Parsons, *History of Rye* (Concord, N.H.: Rumford Printing, 1905), p. 452.

*Portsmouth Journal,* January 12, 1839.

*Portsmouth City Directory 1827.*

156. John Frost, *New Castle Record Book,* p. 11.

157. Stackpole, *Old Kittery and Her Families*, pp. 793–794.

158. *Portsmouth Journal,* November 9, 1839.

159. Folsom, *Genealogy of The Folsom Family In Two Volumes,* Vol. I: 200.

160. M. A. Stickney, *The Fowler Family, 1883.*

*Portsmouth City Directory 1834* and *1839–40.*

161. Stackpole, *Old Kittery and Her Families,* pp. 443–447.

162. Currier Family Bible in collections of the Portsmouth Historical Society.

Frost, *Portsmouth Record Book Vol. I,* p. 164.

# Bibliography

Adams, Nathaniel. *Annals of Portsmouth*. C. Norris, 1825.

Alden, Rev. Timothy, Jr. "A Discourse Delivered before the members of the Portsmouth Female Asylum ... 16 September, 1804." Portsmouth: J. Melcher, 1804.

————. "The Glory of America—A Century Sermon." Portsmouth: William Treadwell & Co., 1801.

Bolton, Ethel Stanwood and Coe, Eva Johnston. *American Samplers*. Boston: The Colonial Dames of America in the State of Massachusetts, 1921.

Brewster, Charles W. *Rambles About Portsmouth, Sketches of Persons, Localities, and Incidents of Two Centuries*. Portsmouth: C. W. Brewster & Son, Series I 1859, Series II 1869.

Buckminster, Joseph. "A Discourse Delivered before the Members of the Portsmouth Female Charity School." Portsmouth: W. Pierce, 1803.

Burroughs, Charles. "An Address on Female Education, Delivered in Portsmouth, N.H. October 26, 1827."

Colby, Averil. *Samplers*. London: B. T. Batsford, 1964.

Cott, Nancy F. *The Bonds of Womanhood, Women's Sphere in New England, 1780–1835*. New Haven: Yale University Press, 1977.

Davidson, Mary M. *Plimoth Colony Samplers*. Marion, MA: The Channings, 1974.

DePauw, Linda Grant and Hunt, Conover. *Remember the Ladies: Women in America 1750–1815*. An exhibition catalog. New York: Viking Press in Association with the Pilgrim Society, 1976.

Deutsch, Davida Tenenbaum. "Samuel Folwell of Philadelphia: An Artist for the Needleworker." *Antiques* 119, No. 2 (February 1981): 420–423.

———. "Washington Memorial Prints." *Antiques* 111, No. 2 (February 1977): 324–331.

——— and Ring, Betty. "Homage to Washington in Needlework and Prints." *Antiques* 119, No. 2 (February 1981): 402–419.

Dexter, E. G. *History of Education in the U.S.* New York: Macmillan, 1919.

Dexter, F. B. *Diary of David McClure.* New York: 1899.

Edmonds, Mary Jane. *Samplers and Samplermakers.* New York: Rizzoli, Los Angelos County Museum of Art, 1991.

———. "Samplers." *Century* 83, No. 5 (March 1912): 676–685.

Foster, Joseph. *Colonel Joseph Foster, His Children and Grandchildren.* Hartford, CT: Edition of Four Copies, 1935.

Garrett, Elizabeth Donaghy. "American Samplers and Needlework Pictures in the DAR Museum. Part I 1739–1806." *Antiques* 105, No. 2 (February 1974): 356–364.

———. "American Samplers and Needlework Pictures in the DAR Museum. Part II 1806–1840." *Antiques* 107, No. 4 (April 1975): 688–701.

———. "The Theodore H. Kapnek Collection of American Samplers." *Antiques* 114, No. 3 (September 1978): 540–559.

Giffen, Jane C. "Susanna Rowson and Her Academy." *Antiques* 98, No. (September 1970): 436–440.

Harbeson, Georgiana Brown. *American Needlework.* New York: Coward-McCann, 1938.

Huish, Marcus B. *Samplers and Tapestry Embroideries.* New York: Longmans, Green & Co., 1913.

Keith, Elmer D. "Architectural Sidelights from Samplers." *Antiques* 57, No. 6 (June 1950): 437–439.

Kerber, Linda K. *Women of the Republic, Intellect and Ideology in Revolutionary America.* Chapel Hill, NC: University of North Carolina Press, 1980.

King, Donald. *Samplers, Victoria and Albert Museum.* London: Her Majesty's Stationery Office, 1960.

Krueger, Glee F. *A Gallery of American Samplers: The Theodore H. Kapnek Collection.* New York: E. P. Dutton in Association with the Museum of American Folk Art, 1978.

———. *New England Samplers to 1840.* Old Sturbridge Village, Sturbridge, MA., 1978.

Lane, Rose Wilder. *Woman's Day Book of American Needlework*. New York: Simon & Schuster, 1963.

Little, Nina Fletcher. *Little By Little*. New York: E. P. Dutton, 1984.

Lockridge, Kenneth A. *Literacy in Colonial New England*. New York: Norton Co., 1974.

New Hampshire Historical Society. *The Decorative Arts of New Hampshire: A Sesquicentennial*. Concord: Exhibition catalog, June 28 to September 29, 1973.

————. "History in Needlework." *Historical New Hampshire* (April 1946): 9–13.

Nylander, Jane. "Some Print Sources of New England Schoolgirl Art." *Antiques* 110, No. 2 (August 1976): 292–301.

Ogden, John Cosens. *The Female Guide or Thoughts on the Education of that Sex Accommodated to the State of Society, Manners and Government in the United States*. Concord, NH: George Hough, 1793.

Prouty, Dwight L. "The Spectator. A Loan Exhibition of Embroidered Pictures and Samplers." Boston: *The Outlook* (November 29, 1913).

Ring, Betty. *American Needlework Treasures*. New York: E. P. Dutton, 1987.

————. "Checklist of Looking-Glass and Frame Makers and Merchants Known by Their Labels." *Antiques* 129, No. 5 (May 1981): 1178–1195.

————. *Girlhood Embroidery, American Samplers and Pictorial Needlework, 1650-1850, Vols. I and II*. New York: Alfred A. Knopf, 1993.

————. *Let Virtue Be A Guide to Thee, Needlework in the Education of Rhode Island Women 1730–1830*. Providence, RI: A catalog for an exhibition at the Rhode Island Historical Society, 1983.

————. "Memorial Embroideries by American Schoolgirls." *Antiques* 100, No. 4 (October 1971): 570–575.

————. "Mrs. Saunders' and Miss Beach's Academy, Dorchester." *Antiques* 110, No. 2 (August 1976): 302–312.

————. *Needlework—An Historical Survey*. New York: Universe Books, 1975.

————. "Schoolgirl Embroideries: A Credit to the Teachers." *Worcester Art Museum Journal* 5 (1981–82): 18–31.

Schiffer, Margaret B. *Arts and Crafts of Chester County, Pennsylvania*. Exton: Schiffer Publishing Ltd., 1980.

————. *Historical Needlework of Pennsylvania*. New York: Charles Scribner's Sons, 1968.

Schorsch, Anita. *Mourning Art in the New Nation*. Clinton, NJ: The Main Street Press, 1976.

———. "A Key to the Kingdom: The Iconography of a Mourning Picture." *Winterthur Portfolio* 14, No. 1 (Spring 1979).

Sprague, Laura Fecych et al. *Agreeable Situations, Society, Commerce, and Art in Southern Maine, 1780–1830*. Boston: Northeastern University Press, 1987.

Swan, Susan Burrows. *Plain & Fancy: American Women and Their Needlework, 1700–1850*. New York: Holt, Rinehart and Winston, 1977.

———. *Winterthur Guide to American Needlework*. New York: A Winterthur Book, Crown Publishers, 1976.

Ulrich, Laurel Thatcher. *Good Wives: Image and Reality in the Lives of Women in Northern New England 1650–1750*. New York: Alfred A. Knopf, 1982.

Winslow Anna Green,. *Diary of Anna Green Winslow, a Boston Schoolgirl*, Alice Morse Earle, ed. Boston and New York: Houghton, Mifflin and Co. The Riverside Press, Cambridge, 1894.

Woody, Thomas. *A History of Women's Education in the United States*. New York: Science Press, 1929.

Worthley, Mary Genn. *History of Private Schools of Portsmouth, N.H. 1763–1800*. Washington, DC: Master's Thesis at the George Washington University, Feb. 22, 1938.

W. P. A. *Hands That Built New Hampshire*. Brattleboro, VT: Vermont Printing Co., 1940.

# *Index*

# About the Authors

**John F. LaBranche** received his bachelor of arts degree from the University of New Hampshire in 1977. He served on the staff of Strawbery Banke Museum for eight years, first as registrar and subsequently as curator. He also served as curator at the Old York Historical Society in York, Maine, for five years. He currently divides his time between an interior design business in Maine and working as a textile stylist for Malden Mills Industries in Lawrence, Massachusetts.

**Rita F. Conant** received her bachelor of arts degree from Connecticut College for Women in 1945 and a master of science degree from Teachers College at Columbia University in 1950. She has worked as a research instructor at Harvard School of Public Health, spent countless hours in volunteer capacities performing research for the Concord Antiquarian Society in Concord, Massachusetts, and currently serves as curator of the Portsmouth Athenaeum.